BIRD SPOTTING

JOHN HOLLAND

Illustrated by Rein Stuurman

BLANDFORD PRESS
POOLE   DORSET

First Published	1955
Second Edition	1959
(revised and enlarged)	
Reprinted (with additions)	1963
Reprinted (with additions and	1965
revisions)	
Fifth Revised Edition	1970
Reprinted	1973
Reprinted	1976

ISBN 0 7137 0334 2

INTRODUCTION

THE ability to recognise most of the birds which are known in the British Isles must be acquired gradually; it is a painstaking business, though one that will never be dull or tiresome. The *Handbook of British Birds* gives descriptions of no less than 520 birds. But there are a number of rarities among them, which may never be seen in a lifetime.

P. A. D. Hollom has, in his *Popular Handbook of British Birds*, excluded all birds which have been seen less than ten or a dozen times in the British Isles. Nevertheless, his book still deals with 330 species (some of which are only subspecies). And if we know that in many of them the females differ considerably from the males, and that the young have yet a different plumage, we can realise how wide is our subject.

However, the charm of bird study will already be within our reach, when we come to know a hundred or so at first sight.

An experienced ornithologist is able to tell the Greenshank from the Redshank, even if he sees the bird only for a few moments. This is possible mainly because he knows at first sight to which Order, or even Family the bird seen belongs. And furthermore he knows what to look for; length, colour and perhaps a slight tilt of the bill, the pattern of the white patches on back and wings, the presence of bars on the tail and other such particulars that may seem trivialities.

The bird watcher's aim should be to classify the bird as soon as he sees it. That is to say, it will not always be possible to call it at once by its name, but at least to place it in its group.

It is possible to group the birds on the British List according to various systems, but I believe that the best and most satisfactory classification is the scientific one, as it was first conceived by the great Swedish biologist Carl von Linné (Linnaeus) in the eighteenth century. This is a classification based largely on anatomical relationship, which in most cases goes together with likeness in appearance and posture. For instance, a knowledge of our common Wagtails enables the bird watcher, when seeing one of the rare ones, to know that this is a Wagtail also.

The scheme Carl von Linné put forward (and it has often been rearranged although the principles remain) is quite precise. The Animal Kingdom is divided into Classes, of which the birds form one Class. This Class is divided into Orders. These Orders are divided into Families. There are still further divisions which we will not deal with here. The most important help to bird recognition is the ability to tell at once to which Order, or even to which Family, or Genus a bird belongs when we encounter it for the first time. The birds on the British List belong to eighteen Orders:

Gaviiformes

Procellariiformes

Podicipediformes

Pelecaniformes

Ciconiiformes
Anseriformes
Falconiformes
Galliformes
Gruiformes
Charadriiformes
Columbiformes

Cululiformes
Strigiformes
Caprimulgiformes
Apodiformes
Coraciiformes
Piciformes
Passeriformes

The aim of this series of books is to introduce some of the birds of these Orders by giving their portraits in picture as well as in words. Not only is their Order given in each case, but also their Family.

When you come to know a few species well, you will be able to classify birds unknown to you in the Order or the Family to which they belong.

The selection I have made for these books is, of course, arbitrary, and you may miss some birds that are seen in your district. You may also think that others which I have included might have been left out. However, the area dealt with is very extensive and a bird that is common in the south may be rare, or even unknown, in the north. By confining the compass of this volume to some 230 specimens, we have avoided the confusion that often befalls the beginner when he turns to books of great details, and including all known species of British birds.

The limits of a pocket-size book naturally restrict the detail of the descriptions, but I have endeavoured to give as many of the essentials as possible. It is for this reason also, that I have often given only a description of the male, as the descriptions of females and young would have taken too much of the space necessary for other particulars. I have given the sizes of the birds in order that a comparison may be made with other birds already known to the reader. I use terms like "Sparrow-sized" or "about Mallard-size", which I hope convey the right impressions.

Of the birds breeding in the British Isles, particulars are also given about the site of the nest, number of eggs, and breeding-season. There is also a short summary of distribution.

At the end of each caption are given the Latin (Lat.) names, the knowledge of which comes very useful when talking with ornithologists from abroad or reading foreign bird-books, as they are used all over the world. As most ornithologists love to travel abroad to study species that are scarce or unknown in Britain, the names of the species dealt with are given for some of the surrounding countries: Holland (D.), France (F.), Germany (G.) and Sweden (S.). When differing from the English names, the names used in the United States of America (N.Am.) are also given.

This volume is divided into six parts following the pattern of the original publication in six volumes.

Note: See Appendix page 284 for a new approach to classification.

1

Pheasants rocketing into the air

FAMILIES REPRESENTED
IN PART 1

Gaviidae	Divers
Podicipitidae	Grebes
Procellariidae	Petrels
Sulidae	Gannet
Phalacrocoracidae	Cormorants
Ardeidae	Herons
Ciconiidae	Stork
Threskiornithidae	Spoonbill
Phasianidae	Pheasants
Tetraonidae	Grouse
Rallidae	Rails
Scolopacidae	Sandpipers

SPOONBILLS

DIVERS TO GAME BIRDS

THIS part deals with eight of the Orders of birds on the British List (see page 4). The (Latin) names of these Orders for the moment may be only words, but when it is learnt that Gaviiformes stands for Divers, Podicipediformes for Grebes, Procellariiformes for Petrels, Pelecaniformes for Gannet and Cormorants, Ciconiiformes for the Heron-tribe, Galliformes for Game Birds and Gruiformes for the Rail family which includes such birds as Moorhen and Coot, the student begins to get the point.

The Great Crested Grebe in summertime is a very conspicuous bird, quite common in most countries. Of the Petrels the Fulmar is rapidly spreading along our coasts from the North. Along the coasts we may also see Gannet, Cormorant and Shag. Of the Ciconiiformes the Heron is the commonest and accordingly known even by those who have never paid special attention to birds.

The Game Birds include those residents of the North Country and Scotland, the Red Grouse, Capercaillie and Ptarmigan. These birds of course are mostly local. The Woodcock, belonging to the Charadiiformes is given here.

Gruiformes have representatives in every inland area where water is to be found.

RED-THROATED DIVER

About as big (59 cm*) as Mallard, pointed tip-tilted bill. In summer: red throat and grey crown. In winter: palest of Divers, the dark back being sprinkled with small white spots. No wing-bar. Sexes alike.

Nests mostly along quite small tarns; 2 (3) eggs; May/June. Both sexes incubate (24-29 d.); young tended by both parents (often for 2 m.). Single-brooded.

Breeds in Scottish Highlands and islands and (in one locality only) NW. Ireland. Winter visitor along all coasts.

*23 in.

Lat. Gavia stellata / N. Am. Red-throated Loon / D. Roodkeelduiker / F. Plongeon catmarin / G. Nordseetaucher / S. Smålom

12

GREAT CRESTED GREBE

Largest grebe (48 cm*) with long slender neck. In summer: long crest and rufous collar. In winter: crest less obvious, collar hardly visible. Sexes alike. Dives often.

Nests on weeds near bank of river or lake; 3-4 eggs; Apr./Aug. Both sexes incubate (28 d.) and manage young for about 10 w. Single-(double-) brooded.

Resident, although breeding-population was reduced by plume-trade to below 50 pairs in 1860; protection raised this number to more than a thousand pairs in 1931 and perhaps more than double this figure at present.

*19 in.

Lat. Podiceps cristatus | D. Fuut | F. Grèbe huppé | G. Haubentaucher | S. Skäggdopping

Order *PODICIPEDIFORMES*   Family *PODICIPITIDAE*
RED-NECKED GREBE

Smaller (43 cm*) than Great Crested. In summer: chestnut neck, no head-ornaments. In winter: no stripe over eye, bill black and yellow, dark crown reaching down below the eyes, gradually merging into white of cheeks. Sexes alike.
Winter visitor, mainly to E. coast.   *17 in.

Lat. Podiceps griseigena / N. Am. Holboell's Grebe / D. Roodhalsfuut / F. Grèbe jougris / G. Rothalstaucher / S. Gråhakedopping

SLAVONIAN GREBE

Rather small (33 cm*). In summer: black cheeks and ear-tufts pointing upwards, neck, breast and flanks chestnut. In winter: dark crown reaching down to eye level and contrasting sharply with white of cheeks. Short straight dark bill with whitish tip. Sexes alike.
Floating nest of weeds and mud along little bays, sometimes semi-social; 3-5 eggs; May/July. Both sexes incubate (20-25 d.) and manage young for about 5 w. Single- (double-) brooded.
Rather scarce resident in Inverness and Sutherland; winter visitor to all coasts.

Lat. Podiceps auritus / N. Am. Horned Grebe / D. Kuifduiker / F. Grèbe esclavon / G. Ohrentaucher / S. Svarthakedopping
                                                   *13 in.

BLACK-NECKED GREBE

Small (30 cm*) grebe with slightly uptilted bill. In winter: dark of crown extends below eye. Sexes alike. Social breeder in shallow water; 3-4 eggs; May/July. Both sexes incubate (20-21 d.) and manage young for about 4-5 w. Often double-brooded.
Resident, breeding irregularly in most parts of British Isles; winter visitor to E. and S. coast of England.

Lat. Podiceps nigricollis / N. Am. Eared Grebe / D. Geoorde fuut / F. Grèbe à cou noir / G. Schwarzhalstaucher /. S. Svarthalsad dopping

14   *12 in.

LITTLE GREBE

Smallest (25 cm*) grebe. In summer: White patch near short black bill, dark brown head with chestnut cheeks. In winter: brown and buff, not black and white. Sexes alike.

Nest (often floating) built of water-weeds by both sexes; 4-6 eggs; Apr./June. Both sexes incubate (19-20 d.); young fed by both parents. Double-brooded.

Resident in Britain, though rare in N. Scotland and only winter visitor to Shetlands. Most birds seem to move to coastal waters in winter, but no true migration. Winter visitor from Continent.

*10 in.

Lat. Podiceps ruficollis | Also: Dabchick | D. Dodaars | F. Grèbe castagneux | G. Zwergtaucher | S. Smådopping

FULMAR PETREL

Gull-like bird (45 cm*). Big head and thick neck and proportionately narrow wings (without black tips) in combination with sailing on stiff wings preclude possibility of confusion with members of gull-tribe. Light and dark colour-phases. Sexes alike.

Social breeder on coastal cliffs; 1 egg; May/June. Both sexes incubate (8 w.) and manage young for about 8 w. Single-brooded.

More or less resident, though nesting-colonies are left in second half of August, but re-occupation often starts as soon as early November. Until 1878 St Kilda was only breeding station in British Isles but since then the Fulmar has rapidly colonised along British coasts.

*18 in.

Lat. Fulmarus glacialis | D. Noordse stormvogel | F. Pétrel fulmar | G. Eissturmvogel | S. Stormfågel

MANX SHEARWATER

A sea bird (36 cm*) with black plumage above and white underneath.
Strong flight, skimming above the water with straight stiff wings.
Social breeder on coastal cliffs; nest in hole in the turf; 1 egg; May/June.
More or less resident and breeds mostly on the west coast of the British
Isles; visits many parts of the coasts in the latter part of the year.
Very active at breeding place at night and has a weird cry or wail.

Lat. Puffinus puffinus
D. Noordse pijlstormvogel
F. Puffin des Anglais
G. Schwarzschnabel Sturm-
taucher
S. Mindra lira

*16 in.

Above: Manx Shearwater
Below: Storm Petrel

17

STORM PETREL

An ocean bird (15 cm*), coming to land only for nesting and when storm driven. Brownish-black plumage with white band above the tail.
Breeds on the north-west coast of British Isles; nest in a hole in the turf or a crevice in rock; one egg; June.
Colour picture page 17
LEACH'S PETREL (20 cm**) is larger and has a forked tail.

*6½ in.   **8½ in.

Lat. Hydrobates pelagicus | D. Stormvogeltje | F. Thalaissidrome tempête |
G. Sturmschwalbe | S. Stormsvala

GANNET

Very large (90 cm*), all-white with black-tipped wings. Dives head-first into sea often from 100 ft. Grey-brown young birds are easily recognised by typical gannet-shape. Sexes alike.

Social breeder on cliffs of marine islands; 1 egg; Apr./May. Both sexes incubate (43-45 d.) and manage young. Singled-brooded.

J. Fisher (1947) states that in 1939 there were about 109,000 breeding adults in 12 colonies in the British Isles (St Kilda 16,900, Little Skellig 9500, Grassholm 6000, Ailsa Craig 5419 and Bass Rock 4374 occupied nest sites). Seen inland only after gales.

*36 in.

Lat. Sula bassana | Also: Solan Goose | D. Jan van Gent | F. Fou de Bassan/ G. Basstölpel | S. Havssula

SHAG

Smaller (75 cm*) than Cormorant, all-black. In summer has recurved crest. Immature birds have white chin but little or no white on breast. Sexes alike.

Social breeder on cliff-ledges; 3-4 eggs; Apr./June. Incubation by both sexes (35 d.) Both sexes manage young for about 7 w. Single- (double-) brooded.

Rather the same distribution as Cormorant, though Shag does not breed in northern England, nor along Cardigan Bay. Never breeds inland like Cormorant does in a few places.

*30 in.

Lat. Phalacrocorax aristotelis / *D. Kuifaalscholver* / *F. Cormoran huppé* / *G. Krähenscharbe* / *S. Toppskarv*

CORMORANT

Big (90 cm*) long-necked black bird. In summer: white cheek and thigh-patch. No crest. Immature birds have dull white under-parts. Sexes alike.

Social breeder on rocky islands and cliff-ledges along the coast; occasionally (Ireland) in trees; 3-4 eggs; Apr./June. Both sexes incubate (26-29 d.) and manage young for about 5 weeks. Usually single-brooded.

Resident, commonly breeding along W. coasts of British Isles (not in the Firth of Forth or along most parts of W. Highland coast) and locally along E. coast.

*36 in.

Lat. Phalacrocorax carbo | N. Am. European Cormorant | D. Aalscholver | F. Cormoran ordinaire | G. Kormoran | S. Storskarv

21

HERON

Well-known very large (90 cm*) grey, long-necked and long-legged bird; in flight broad, rounded wings, neck drawn in and legs showing behind tail. Sexes alike. Young have no black on crown.

Social breeder in trees and sometimes on cliffs. Female builds nest, male bringing sticks etc.; 3-5 eggs, Feb./June. Both sexes incubate (25 d.) and feed young. (Usually) single-brooded.

Breeding population of England and Wales in 1952: 3017 pairs. Scotland and Ireland have also (mostly smaller) heronries. Passage-migrants and winter visitors from the Continent. British birds do not migrate.

*36 in.

Lat. Ardea cinerea / D. Blauwe reiger / F. Héron cendré / G. Fischreiher / S. Grå häger

LITTLE BITTERN

Smallest of heron-tribe (35 cm*); male with conspicuous white patch on wing, sharply contrasting with black on rest of wing and back; female has brown wings and back, on which light patch is less obvious.

Rare vagrant that has been recorded in nearly all counties of England and Wales, most times from Apr./June and from Aug./Oct. Breeding is said to have occurred in E. Anglia but has never been proven. Secretive crepuscular bird, haunting reed-beds and reeds fringing rivers and meres.

*14 in.

Lat. Ixobrychus minutus | D. Woudaapje | F. Blongios nain | G. Zwergrohr-dommel | S. Dvärgrördrom

BITTERN

Large (75 cm*) golden-brown bird with long pointed bill and relatively short legs. Seldom observed on the wing, except when feeding young, owing to largely crepuscular habits.

Nests in vast reed-beds; 4-6 eggs; Apr./May. Only female breeds (25-26 d.) and manages young, which leave nest after 16-20 days but are fully fledged only after about 8 w. Single-brooded. The male Bittern shows polygamous tendencies.

Resident, breeding regularly in E. Anglia, recently also in Lincs. and Kent. Perhaps also elsewhere in extensive reedbeds of swamps and fens. In winter time wandering birds may be seen in other parts.

*30 in.

Lat. Botaurus stellaris / D. Roerdomp / F. Butor étoilé / G. Grosse Rohrdommel / S. Rördrom

24

Order CICONIIFORMES
Family CICONIIDAE

WHITE STORK

Well-known bird (100cm) from fairy books, easily identified by long red legs and red bill (young birds have black bills and brownish-red legs), white plumage and black wings. In flight outstretched neck and legs trailing behind.

Continental birds may be seen from March/June and in autumn in E. and S. England, though even there seldom; very scarce elsewhere.

The European population seems to be decreasing rapidly at present, though there had been a remarkable increase from 1930 till 1940.

Lat. Ciconia ciconia | D. Ooievaar | F. Cigogne blanche | G. Weiszer Storch | S. Vit stork

Family THRESKIORNI-THIDAE

SPOONBILL (see page 10)

Slightly smaller (85 cm**) than Heron. White colouring and spoon-shaped black bill are very distinctive. In flight neck and (black) legs are stretched out. Rather gregarious.

Regular visitor to E. Anglia and most parts of S. coast of England from Apr. to Nov. Rare vagrant elsewhere.

Lat. Platalea leucorodia | D. Lepelaar | F. Spatule blanche | G. Löffelreiher | S. Skedstork

*40 in.   **34 in.   25

PARTRIDGES
Showing their effective camouflage

PARTRIDGE

Small (30 cm*) rotund bird with rufous tail and chestnut patch on breast in shape of horse-shoe (often almost absent in older females). Whirring flight when taking off is another characteristic of this small game-bird.

Nest is shallow hollow scraped by female, lined with dry grasses and leaves; 10-20 eggs; Apr./May. Incubation (23-25 d.) by female only. Young leave nest within few hours of hatching and are tended by both parents. Families keep together long afterwards in "coveys" Single-brooded (See also page 48).

Common resident in most counties of England and Wales; breeds locally in Scotland and rather scarce in Ireland.

Lat. Perdix perdix | N. Am. Hungarian Partridge | D. Patrijs | F. Perdrix grise | G. Rebhuhn | S. Rapphöna

The **Red-legged Partridge** (Alectoris rufa) is slightly larger (34 cm**) and has red bill and legs, white cheeks and throat, and flanks barred with white, black and chestnut. This resident in S. and E. England was introduced (from France) in the 18th century.

*12 in. **13½ in.

QUAIL

This miniature partridge(18 cm*)is much less gregarious than the Partridge, though family-parties may keep together, even on migration. Sexes almost alike.

Nest is little hollow scraped by female; 7-12 eggs; May/June. Only female broods (16-21 d.); young leave nest almost immediately and fly well within 3 weeks. They are managed by female only. Single-brooded.

Most quails arrive in May. Mostly confined to S. England, scarce in E. Scotland and E. Ireland.

*7 in.

Lat. Coturnix coturnix | D. Kwartel | F. Caille | G. Wachtel | S. Vaktel

PHEASANT

Game bird (up to 90 cm*) with plumage of chestnut-brown, beautifully marked with green, purple and cream. Bright red face. Hen bird is less handsome and has a mottle-brown plumage.

Nest on ground lined with grass and leaves. 10-14 eggs; April/June.

Resident in most parts of the British Isles, especially on game preserved land. Prefers wooded land, bushes and scrub. Mainly runs but will rocket upwards a great speed when startled (See page 8).

*36 in.

Lat. Phasianus colchicus / D. Fazant / F. Faisan / G. Fasan / S. Fasan

Order GALLIFORMES   *Family TETRAONIDAE*

RED GROUSE

A game bird (38 cm*). Male plumage dark-red-brown heavily barred with black and red wattle over the eye. Female also barred black and buff.

Nest on the ground among the heather, 7/14 eggs; April/May.

Resident; a bird of the moorlands in Northern England and Scotland, living in flocks.

*15 in.

Lat. Lagopus scoticus scoticus | D. Schotse sneeuwhoen | F. Lagopède d'Ecosse | G. Schottisches Moorschneehuhn | S. Moripa

BLACK GROUSE

Also known as Blackgame, Blackcock (male), Greyhen (female).
Larger (50 cm*) than Red Grouse the male has black plumage and a lyre shaped tail with white under tail-coverts, feathered legs and a bright red wattle over eye. Hen and juveniles are brown with mottled and barred markings. Cock has a crowing note.

Nest on ground. 7-12 eggs. April/May.

Resident; breeding on moors in South-West England, Wales, locally in North England and over most of Scotland. Frequents moorlands and woodlands and favours pine and birch trees.

*19¾ in.

Lat. Lyrurus tetrix britannicus / D. Korhoen /F. Tetras à queue fourchue / G. Birkhuhn / S. Orre

Order CHARADRIIFORMES   *Family SCOLOPACIDAE*

SNIPE

Very long bill (6½ cm*) is characteristic as are conspicuous light streaks running down the back and zig-zag flight, combined with harsh cry of flushed birds. Length about 27 cm**. Sexes alike.

Nest on the ground in grassy marshes; 4 (6) eggs; Apr./June. Only female incubates (19-20 d.), but young are tended by both parents. They fly when 2 w. old. Single- (double-) brooded.

           *2½ in. **11 in.

Resident, common breeder throughout the British Isles, though only local in S. England. Snipe from the Continent come to winter in or pass through Britain.

Lat. Gallinago gallinago | N. Am. Wilson's Snipe | D. Watersnip | F. Bécassine ordinaire | G. Bekassine | S. Enkelbeckasin

33

Order *GALLIFORMES*   Family *TETRAONIDAE*

PTARMIGAN

Slightly larger than a partridge, this bird (36 cm*) has a summer plumage of brown, barred with grey and buff, and in winter is snow white except for a few black marks on tail and wings. Both male and female have a red comb over the eye.

Nest on ground in a hollow; 5-9 eggs; May/June; only female incubates (24-26 days), single-brooded.

Resident on high mountains in Northern Scotland and the Western Isles.

*14½ in.

summer ♀

Lat. Lagopus mutus | N. Am. Grand Tetras | D. Sneeuwhoen | F. Lagopède des Alpes | G. Alpen schneehuhn | S. Fjällripa

34

PTARMIGAN
Cock in winter plumage

CAPERCAILLIE

This large bird (85 cm*) of the forests is famous for its nuptial display of spreading tail and wings.

Plumage is black with green on breast, brown tinge on the wings. It has a long red wattle over the eye. Female is smaller (24 ins.) and red-brown mottled with buff, white and black.

Nest on ground; 7-10 eggs; April/May. Only female incubates (27-29 days), single-brooded.

Only found in forests of Scotland.

*34 in.

Lat. Tetrao urogallus / D. Auerhoen / F. Grand Tetras / G. Auerhuhn / S. Tjäder

MOORHEN

Small (32 cm*) almost black waterbird (young olive-brown with whitish throat and belly) with conspicuous white under tail-coverts and white line on flank. No wing bar. Red shield on forehead and red bill with yellow tip. (Young have greenish-brown shield and bill.) Sexes alike. Less gregarious than Coot.

Nest built by both sexes; 6-12 eggs; Apr./July. Incubation by both sexes (19-22 d.); young leave nest after 2-3 d. They are managed by both parents. Double-brooded.

Common resident, breeding along all kinds of fresh waters, even ponds in town-parks, provided adequate cover is present. Some winter visitors arrive on E. coast in autumn.

*13 in.

Lat. Gallinula chloropus | Also: Waterhen | N. Am. Florida Gallinule | D. Waterhoentje | F. Poule d'eau | G. Teichhuhn | S. Rörhöna

COOT

All-black, rather plump waterbird (37 cm*) with white frontal shield and bill and small white wing-bar. Brownish-grey young have white throat and breast. Sexes alike. More gregarious than Moorhen.

Nest built by both sexes; 6-10 eggs; March/May. Incubation by both sexes (21-24 d.); young leave nest within 3-4 days. Each parent manages part of the brood. Double-brooded.

Fairly common resident (locally very common): prefers lakes and large ponds to smaller waters. In winter often associates with ducks.

*15 in.

Lat. Fulica atra | D. Meerkoet | F. Foulque | G. Blässhuhn | S. Sothöna

CORNCRAKE

Also known as LAND-RAIL (26 cm*) this brown bird with dark streaks above and pale under-parts is heard more often than it is seen. Its distinctive call, a harsh "crek, crek" is heard night and day in the breeding season.

Nest on the ground, in grass or sedge; 8-12 eggs; May/June. Incubation by female (14-21 days). Single-brooded.

Summer visitor, breeding in the North of the British Isles and sporadically in local places.

*10 in.

Lat. Crex crex | *D. Kwartelkoning* | *F. Râle des genêts* | *G. Wachtelkönig* | *S. Ängsknarr*

WOODCOCK

Bigger than common Snipe (35 cm*); longer (7 cm**) bill, no light streaks on face or back; round-winged, rufous coloured bird. Sexes alike.

Nest on the ground (often at foot of tree); 4 (6) eggs; Apr./May. Incubation (20-21 d.) by female only, but young are tended by both parents. Double-brooded.

Resident, breeding in varying numbers in England, Wales (scarce), Scotland and Ireland. Many Woodcocks from the Continent winter in Britain.

*14 in. **3 in.

Lat. Scolopax rusticola | D. Houtsnip | F. Bécasse | G. Waldschnepfe | S. Morkulla

WATER-RAIL

A bird of secretive habits (28 cm*) very difficult to observe; it is easily alarmed and conceals itself in the river-side rushes. Chestnut-brown back, streaked black. Face, throat and under parts grey; flanks are barred and bill is red.

Nest in marshy places; eggs 7-12; April/July; both sexes incubate (19-20 days) and tend young. Double-brooded.
Continental visitors in winter.

*11½ in.

Lat. Rallus aquaticus | D. Waterral | F. Râle d'eau | G. Wasserralle | S. Vattenrall

Silver Pheasant

NOTES

THE birds illustrated and described in the foregoing pages 12 to 41 are each of a distinctive character and for the purposes of bird watching could not be more exciting subjects. They are all big or biggish, often handsomely coloured, of distinctive shape and many have an individuality all of their own.

On the other hand, they are mostly birds which are difficult to approach, and they inhabit the wild places or the sea; therefore field glasses are almost a necessity to obtain a satisfactory view, or even it may be that a telescope is desirable where the birds are being watched over water such as would be the case with Divers, Grebes, Cormorants etc.

I have always found a special fascination in water birds; they seem so exciting, and what is more the water itself gives this interest an added relaxation. The Coot and the Moorhen are very numerous in some areas and seem to be fairly rapidly increasing. The Grebes are not so familiar but the Heron may turn up in any place where there is water. One has been known to clear a goldfish pond on the outskirts of London.

If the bird watcher takes his interest seriously he will keep notes of the birds he sees and maybe make rough drawings in order to compare birds he does not recognize with his reference books and illustrations. He will take note of their flight, shape, size, colour and voice, the places they frequent, and their habits. This is the only way of finding out the identity of any unfamiliar bird and a most important rule is to make the notes and the sketches on the spot while the details are fresh in mind.

It is also to be remembered that certain birds are only seen in some districts at special seasons. This is true of a number of the birds in this section which are winter visitors and so can only be seen during that period. However, it is exciting to discover such birds, especially if they are of the rarer types, and generally the birds which live on or by the water can be more easily seen at this season of the year.

There are some birds which may be difficult to see or may never be seen in Britain by the watcher. The stork is an example. However, in these days of much travel when so many go abroad for their holidays, it is possible to visit an area frequented by these birds and enjoy the thrill of seeing one for the first time. The stork is easily and often photographed.

Coming to the Game Birds which are dealt with fairly extensively, they are well worth all the time given to them. The partridges and the pheasant are fascinating to study, while the snipe or the woodcock on the wing have nothing to surpass them in action and speed.

There are a number of pheasants which have been introduced to Britain mainly for ornamental purposes, but which have

Snipe in flight

established themselves in some localities. These include the Golden Pheasant, the Silver Pheasant and the Japanese Pheasant.

Other Game Birds illustrated are purely local and in some cases rare, and are only to be seen in the northern part of the country.

Since the first edition was published it has been found that there is a demand by some readers for those parts of this series of books which deal with the birds mostly seen in the reader's own locality.

This, of course, is understandable but it is not the method to acquire a true knowledge of birds. Part of the thrill of bird watching is to visit new places and see unfamiliar birds. The person who lives in the south will find endless interest in bird life in Scotland and may see some of the rarer local birds dealt with in these pages. Consequently he needs a wider knowledge than that which is confined to his own part of the country.

It must be remembered that birds move about and wander in a remarkable way. They can be influenced and governed by all kinds of conditions, mostly of course seasons and weather.

The practice of ringing birds has shown that few if any individual birds are confined to one locality; even robins may move to another country! So a local bird may be any bird that is there at the moment and my advice is to gain as wide a knowledge as possible for one never knows when it may be put to the test.

WOODCOCK in flight

Covey of Partridges

2

DUCKS TO HAWKS

Mallard rising from water

2

ANSERIFORMES

FALCONIFORMES

FAMILIES REPRESENTED
IN PART 2

Anatidae	Ducks
Accipitridae	Hawks
Falconidae	Falcons

DUCKS TO HAWKS

The order Anseriformes includes Ducks, Swans and Geese. As some of these are domesticated and are to be seen in the farmyard or on ornamental lakes they are familiar to everyone. However the commonly and loosely used term "wild duck" in turn embraces a wide variety of birds with such names as Teal, Wigeon, Pintail, Mallard, Shoveler, Pochard, Smew, etc., and the bird watcher's purpose is to know the distinguishing characteristics and to be able to recognise each one as he sees it. These names should be familiar to all and it is well to recognise that there are a dozen dealt with in these pages.

The geese are winter visitors and so are the Whooper Swan, and Bewick's Swan; they are among they heaviest British birds. The Hawks and Falcons have just a dozen representatives illustrated here. Although some may seem to hold mainly academic interest it may be that some fortunate reader will catch sight of a great rarity and be able to recognise it through being previously acquainted himself with its description and habits.

Order ANSERIFORMES *Family ANATIDAE*

GREY LAG GOOSE

Biggest (75-88 cm*) of "grey" geese, very much like farm-yard geese. Heavy head, stout orange bill (without any black) and flesh coloured legs. Head and neck same shade as body, breast more or less spotted. Sexes alike.

Nest lined with down, among heather; 4-6 (8) eggs; Apr./May. Incubation by female only (27-28 d.), but young are tended by both sexes. They fly when 8 w. old. Single-brooded.

Breeds in N. Scotland and on Hebrides. Otherwise winter visitor (Oct./ March), especially to estuary of Firth of Forth. Scarce or even rare in most places.

*30-35 in.

Lat. Anser anser | D. Wilde gans | F. Oie cendrée | G. Graugans | S. Gràgàs

SHELDUCK

Large (60 cm*) goose-like duck white with black head and patches, chestnut band round fore-part of body, (adults only), bright red bill with (male only) knob at base.

Nest usually in rabbit-burrow: 8-14 (20) eggs; May/June. Incubation by female (4 w.) while male often stands guard; both parents guide young (fly when 6-7 w. old), but often lose control, so one may see parents with up to 30 young birds. Single-brooded.

Resident (though some migrate) along all suitable coasts of Britain. In July/August adult birds from E. coast migrate to North Sea S. of Heligoland, where all Sheld-ducks of Western Europe seem to moult.

*24 in.

Lat. Tadorna tadorna | D. Bergeend | F. Tadorne | G. Brandente | S. Gravand

TUFTED DUCK

Rather small (43 cm*). Drake is all-black but for boldly contrasting white flanks. Small tuft at back of head usually only visable at close range.

Nests quite near water (sometimes socially); 8-12 eggs; May/June. Incubation (23-26 d.) and managing of young by duck only. They fly when about 6 w. old. Single-brooded.

Resident, breeding in most counties but absent from most parts of Wales and W. coast of England and Scotland. Does not breed either in S.E. Ireland. Common passage-migrant and winter visitor.

*17 in.

Lat. Aythya fuligula / D. Kuifeend / F. Fuligule morillon / G. Reiherente / S. Vigg

POCHARD

Smaller (46 cm*) than Mallard. Drake is easily recognised by chestnut-red head, black breast and light grey back and flanks. In flight neither drake nor duck show any white on wings.

Nests in or within few inches of water; 8-10 eggs; Apr./June. Incubation (24-28 d.) and managing of young (7-8 w.) by duck only.

Resident, breeding locally in most counties of Scotland and E. and S. England. Has widespread distribution in winter, when visitors from the Continent come to stay in the British Isles.

*18 in.

Lat. Aythya ferina / D. Tafeleend / F. Fuligule milouin / G. Tafelente / S. Brunand

RED-BREASTED MERGANSER

Looks smaller than Mallard (57 cm*); at once recognisable as saw-billed duck by slender bill. Male has dark-green head with prominent crest, chestnut breast-band and grey flanks. Female has brown head gradually blending into white of neck. Dives often.

Nest in hollows or close cover; 7-12 eggs; May/July. Incubation (28-30 d.) and tending of young by duck only. Single brooded.

Resident, breeding commonly in Scotland (though not in southern counties) and Ireland (scarce in S.E. Ireland). Otherwise winter visitor (Oct./Apr.) to most parts of British coast (seldom on inland waters).

*23 in.

Lat. Mergus serrator / D. Middelste zaagbek / F. Harle huppé / G. Mittel-säger / S. Småskrake

GOOSANDER

Looks about Mallard-size (65 cm*). Slender bill. Male: dark-green head like Merganser, but far less prominent crest; white breast and flanks. Crest of female more prominent than that of male, brown of head sharply defined from white of neck. Dives often.

Nests in hollow trees or holes in the ground; 7-17 eggs; Apr./June. Incubation (34-36 d.) and tending of young by duck only. Single-brooded.

Resident, breeding in Scotland. Elsewhere winter visitor (Oct./Apr.) to inland-waters and estuaries.

*26 in.

Lat. Mergus merganser | N. Am. American Merganser | D. Grote zaagbek | F. Harle bièvre | G. Gänsesäger | S. Storskrake

MALLARD

Slightly smaller (58 cm*) than well-known wild-coloured domestic duck. The sexes differ a lot but have characteristic purple-blue speculum with white bars fore and aft. Gregarious; when ducks are breeding drakes form "bachelor parties". Young birds resemble duck.

Nest always near water, under bushes and often in trees, chosen and lined with down by duck; 10-12 eggs, Apr./June. Duck incubates (28 days) while drake guards territory and sometimes helps manage young. Often double-brooded.

Resident throughout British Isles. Passage-migrants and winter visitors from Continent, Faroe and Iceland.

*24 in.

Lat. Anas platyrhynchos / D. Wilde eend / F. Canard sauvage / G. Stockente / S. Gräsand

TEAL

Small (36 cm*) duck with green and black speculum. Drake with conspi-cuous yellow-buff patch under tail and chestnut head with green, buff-seamed patch round eye. Horizontal white streak on wing over specu-lum.

Nests among heather but also in marshes; 8-10 eggs; Apr./May. Incu-bation (21-22 d.) by female only, but drake often assists in managing young for about 3 w. Single-brooded.

Resident throughout the British Isles, though local in S. England. Part of breeding-population moves S. in autumn to France. Passage-migrants and winter visitors from the Continent.

*14 in.

Lat. Anas crecca | N. Am. European Teal | D. Wintertaling | F. Sarcelle d'hiver | G. Krickente | S. Kricka

WHITE-FRONTED GOOSE

Slightly smaller (65-75 cm*) than Grey Lag. Head and neck same shade as back. Adult with obvious white patch at base of pink or yellow bill, legs orange, breast with black bars. Sexes alike.

Winter visitor (Oct./Apr.). A.a. flavirostris (yellow bill) winters mainly in Ireland and W. Scotland; A.a. albifrons winters along British coast and River Severn; flavirostris breeds in W. Greenland, albifrons in N. Russia, Siberia and arctic N. America. Recognition in the field is possible only under favourable conditions.

*26-30 in.

Lat. Anser albifrons | D. Kolgans | F. Oie rieuse | G. Blässgans | S. Bläsgås

Order ANSERIFORMES   *Family ANATIDAE*

BEAN-GOOSE (above)

Big (70-88 cm*) dark goose with stout orange bill marked with black, legs orange. Sexes alike.

Winter visitor (Oct./Apr.) to S. W. Scotland, Northumberland and E. Anglia. Scarce elsewhere. Breeds in northern parts of Scandinavia, Finland, Russia and Siberia.   *28-35 in.

Lat. Anser fabalis | D. Rietgans | F. Oie sauvage | G. Saatgans | S. Sädgås

PINK-FOOTED GOOSE

Smaller than Grey Lag and Bean-goose (62-75 cm*) with dark head and neck, contrasting with rather pale body. Small bill, black with pink band and pink legs. No black on under-parts. Sexes alike.

Winter visitor (Sept./Apr.) mainly to E. coast of England and Scotland, being rather scarce or even rare at most other places but for coast N. of Severn estuary. Breeds in Greenland, Iceland and Spitsbergen. *24-30 in.

Lat. Anser brachyrhynchus | D. Kleine rietgans | F. Oie à bec court | G. Kurz-schnabelgans | S. Spetbergsgås

BRENT GOOSE

Small (55-60 cm*) goose with head, neck (adults with small white patch) and breast black, upper-parts dark grey, vent and tail-coverts white. Sexes alike.

Common winter visitor (Oct./March) to E. coast, local on W. coast and in Wales. Birds with pale breasts (belonging to the race B. b. hrota) seen in Scotland (but for S.E.parts) and Ireland breed in Spitsbergen, Greenland and N.E. Canada. The dark-breasted race breeds in N. Russia and N.W. Siberia.

*22-24 in.

Lat. Branta bernicla | N. Am. Brant | D. Rotgans | F. Bernache cravant | G. Ringelgans | S. Prutgås

WIGEON

Smaller (45 cm*) than Mallard. Drake has chestnut head with conspicuous yellow forehead and crown. White patch on front of wing and on belly make identification of flying birds easy.

Nests among heather on moorland; 7-8 eggs; May/June. Incubation (24-25 d.) by duck only; drake usually guards family. Young fly at about 6 w. Single-brooded.

Resident in Scotland (rather scarce in the South) and N. England. Breeds exceptionally in E. and S.E. England, Wales and Ireland. Common passage-migrant and winter visitor.

*Lat. Anas penelope | Also: Whew, Whistler |
N. Am. European Widgeon | D. Smient |
F. Canard siffleur | G. Pfeifente | S. Bläsand*

*18 in.

Above: Pintail; Below Left: Scaup-Duck; Below Right: Wigeon.

SHOVELER

Somewhat smaller (50 cm*) than Mallard. Duck as well as drake easily recognisable by enormous spatulate bill. Shoveler and Pintail are only drakes with white breasts.

Nests usually in moorland or meadows near water; 8-12 eggs; Apr./May. Only duck incubates (23-25 d.). Drake occasionally assists in guarding of young that fly after about 6 w. Single-brooded.

Resident, breeding in varying numbers in most parts of the British Isles. Common passage-migrant and winter visitor.

*20 in.

Lat. Anas clypeata | Also: Spoonbill | D. Slobeend | F. Canard souchet | G. Löffelente | S. Skedand

SMEW

Small (40 cm*) slender-billed duck. Drake: pure white with black patch round eye and few black streaks at back. In flight shows a surprising amount of black on wings and back. Dives often.

Wintervisitor (Nov./Apr.) to inland waters of S.E. England. Scarce elsewhere, especially in Scotland and Ireland. Breeds in arctic N.W. Europe and N. Asia.

*16 in.

Lat. Mergus albellus | Also: White Nun (drake) | D. Nonnetje | F. Harle piette | G. Zwergsäger | S. Salskrake

69

PINTAIL

About Mallard-size (59 cm*). Long slender neck, long pointed tail in combination with white breast and white band along neck make drake Pintail easily recognisable. Nests on islands in lakes; 7-9 eggs; May/June. Only duck breeds (21-23 days). Drake occasionally assists in guarding of young that fly after about 6 w. Single-brooded.

Resident in Scotland, though breeding only sporadically in southern parts. Elsewhere irregular breeding-bird. Regular though local passage-migrant and winter visitor, mainly along the coast. Colour picture page 67

Lat. Anas acuta / D. Pijlstaart / F. Canard pilet / G. Spiessente / S. Stärtand

*22 in.

SCAUP-DUCK

Smaller (47 cm*) than Mallard. Drake seems to be black with white flanks and grey back. Duck has broad white band round base of bill.

Nests near water; 7-10 eggs; May/June. Incubation (27-28 d.) and managing of young by duck only. They fly when 5-6 w. old. Single-brooded.

Common passage-migrant and winter visitor (Oct./Apr.) to all coasts. Has bred in O. Hebrides, Sutherland and Caithness.
Colour picture page 67   *19 in.

Lat. Aythya marila / N. Am. Greater Scaup-duck / D. Topper / F. Fuligule milouinan / G. Bergente / S. Bergand

MUTE SWAN

Very big (150 cm*) white bird with long neck. Truly wild birds cannot be separated in the field from domesticated or semi-wild swans on ponds, lakes and rivers. Orange (not yellow) bill with black knob (biggest in male) at base distinguish Mute Swan from following species. Juveniles are brownish-grey with grey bill.

Big nest built by female, male bringing material; 5-7 (12) eggs; Apr./May. Both sexes incubate (5 w.) and manage young that are fully fledged in about 4 m.; usually families stay together until next spring. Single-brooded.

E. England has originally had real wild population. Now most residents will be semi-wild birds. At Abbotsbury (Dorset) about 200-500 pairs. Perhaps migrants from Baltic countries, Poland and E. Europe winter in Britain.

*60 in.

Lat. Cygnus olor / Also: Cob *(male)*, Pen *(female)*, Cygnet *(young)* / D. *Knobbelzwaan* / F. *Cygne tuberculé* / G. *Höckerschwan* / S. *Knölsvan*

BEWICK'S SWAN

Smaller (120 cm*) than other Swans. Yellow at base of bill rather bluntly ending at nostril (see illustration below). Juveniles greyish-brown with pale grey blacktipped bill. In winter, families stay together.

Winter visitor (Nov./March) to England, Wales and Ireland, especially when severe winters drive them from the IJsselmeer in Holland, where thousands of them winter. Also in small numbers in Scotland. Breeds in arctic Russia and N.W. Asia.

*48 in.

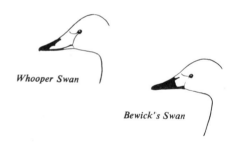

Whooper Swan

Bewick's Swan

Lat. Cygnus bewickii | D. Kleine zwaan | F. Cygne de Bewick | G. Zwergschwan | S. Mindre sångsvan

WHOOPER SWAN

As big (150 cm*) as Mute Swan, but bill yellow at base with black tip. Yellow on bill pointed and reaching beyond nostril (see illustration on page 72). Juveniles brownish with flesh coloured black-tipped bill.

Nest on islands in lakes build by female, male assisting in bringing material; 5-6 eggs; May/June. Incubation by female only (5-6 w.), but young are managed by both parents. They are fully fledged when about 2 m. Single-brooded.

Perhaps few pairs still breed in Scottish Highlands, where present all year round. Otherwise winter visitor (Nov./Apr.) from Iceland and northern parts of Norway, Sweden, Finland, Russia and Asia.

*60 in.

Lat. Cygnus cygnus | Also: Whistling swan | D. Wilde zwaan | F. Cygne sauvage | G Singschwan | S. Sångsvan

Order
FALCONIFORMES

Family ACCIPITRIDAE

BUZZARD

Rather large (50-55 cm*) brown bird of prey, distinctly bigger than crow, broad-winged with relatively short tail. Dark and light colour-phases are confusing, but even very light Buzzards have slightly barred (never white) tail with broad end-bar. Frequent hovering.

Nests in trees and on cliff-ledges along coast and inland; 2-4 eggs; Apr./May. Both sexes incubate (34-38 d.) and manage young, also after they have left the nest when 6-7 w. old. Single-brooded.

Resident, breeding in increasing numbers in S.W. England, Wales,  Lake District, Pennines and most parts of Scotland. Spring and autumn vagrants to Ireland, where exterminated by end of 19th century. On E. coast autumn migrants from N. Europe.

*20-22 in.

Lat. Buteo buteo / D. Buizerd / F. Buse commune / G. Mäusebussard / S Ormvråk

74

BUZZARD

Light colour phase.

MONTAGU'S HARRIER
This illustration shows the long slender wings, black wing tips and the yellow eye of the male.

MONTAGU'S HARRIER

Slightly smaller (39-45 cm*) than Hen-harrier. Male can be separated from that species by dark bar across wings. Has also white patch on rump. Female and young are very difficult to tell from female and young Hen-harriers.

Nest on ground built chiefly by female; 4-5 eggs; May/June. Female breeds for about 30 d. Male brings food to incubating female and young, that fly when about 5 w. old. Single-brooded.

Breeds regularly in E. Anglia and S.W. England, more locally in other parts of England and Wales. Rare vagrant to Scotland and Ireland. Summer visitor from Apr. till second half of Oct.

*15½-18 in.

Lat. Circus pygargus / D. Grauwe kiekendief /F. Busard cendré / G. Wiesenweihe / S. Mindre kärrhök

HOBBY

Slender hawk (30-35 cm*) with Swift-like silhouette. Dark slate-grey upperparts and reddish thighs. Only Peregrine (much bigger) and Hobby have obvious black moustache.

Breeds mostly in old nests of Crows, Magpies; 2-4 eggs; June/July. Incubation mainly by female (28 d.). Male brings food for young but female later assists in hunting. Young leave nest when 4-5 w. old.
Single-brooded.

Summer visitor (Apr./Sept.) breeding as far N. as Cheshire and Yorkshire in small numbers Otherwise rather rare vagrant.

*12-14 in.

Lat. Falco subbuteo | D. Boomvalk | F. Faucon hobereau | G. Baumfalke | S. Lärkfalk

SPARROW-HAWK

Rather small (27-37 cm*) bird of prey of hawk-type. Long tail and short broad wings are typical in combination with habit of lightning dashes along borders of woods and hedgerows when hunting. Under-parts barred. Male smaller than (browner) female.

Nest in trees (near trunk), often built by female only, though male

may assist; 4-5 eggs; May/June. Incubation (always?) by female only (32-35 d.). Male brings prey that is distributed to the young by female. Young leave nest when about 4 w. old. Single-brooded.

Rather common resident in wooded districts, very scarce in N. Scotland. Passage of migrants from the Continent along E. coast in autumn and spring.

*11-15 in.

Lat. Accipiter nisus / D. Sperwer / F. Epervier (ordinaire) / G. Sperber / S. Sparvhök

Order FALCONIFORMES   *Family ACCIPITRIDAE*

MARSH-HARRIER (above)

Long-tailed, long-winged rusty-brown hawk (47-55 cm*), often flying low over reed-beds of marshes and swamps. Though old males may have greyish-brown tails there is never a white patch on rump.

Nest on ground in reed-beds, built by female; 4-5 (7) eggs; Apr./June. Incubation largely by female (35-38 d.) Male brings food for young, that is fed to them by female. They leave the nest after 5-6 w. but are fully fledged only 3 w. after. Single-brooded.

(read on)

80   *19-22 in.

HEN-HARRIER

Typical harrier (42-51 cm*) with white patch on rump. Male light greyish-blue, without dark bar on dark-tipped wings. Female and juveniles brown, but also with light patch on rump.

Nest on ground, chiefly built by female; 4-5 eggs; May/June. Only female broods (30 d.). Male brings food that female distributes to young which fly when 5-6 w. old. Single-brooded.

Breeds in the Orkneys, E. Hebrides (few) and in Scottish Highlands, perhaps also in Ireland. Occasionally in Wales and England. Otherwise passage-migrant and winter visitor from Continent.

Lat. Circus cyaneus | N. Am. Marsh Hawk | D. Blauwe kiekendief | F. Busard St Martin | G. Kornweihe | S. Blå kärrhök

*17-20 in.

(c o n t i n u e d)

Rare wanderer outside breeding-season, breeding in Norfolk, Suffolk, N. Wales in very small numbers.

Lat. Circus aeruginosus | D. Bruine kiekendief | F. Busard des roseaux | G. Rohrweihe | S. Brun kärrhök

PEREGRINE FALCON

Robust falcon (38-48 cm*). In flight: long pointed wings and rather short tail. Female birds are distinctly bigger than Kestrel and Hobby. Black moustache and slate-grey upper-parts like Hobby, which has reddish thighs. (Rufous-mantled) Kestrel has longer tail as has Sparrow-Hawk, which has rather short, broad wings. Female Peregrine (bigger) is usually darker than male.

Nest on cliffs (seldom in trees); 3-4 eggs; Apr./May. Incubation by both sexes (28-29 d.). Young, tended by both parents, fly when 5-6 w. old. Single-brooded.

Resident and passage-migrant breeding in decreasing numbers in mountainous and hilly districts and on sea-cliffs.

*15-19 in.

Lat. Falco peregrinus /N. Am. Duck Hawk / D. Slechtvalk / F. Faucon pélerin / G. Wanderfalke / S. Pilgrimsfalk

82

MERLIN

Smallest (25-32 cm*) falcon, male about
Throstle-size. Upper-parts slate-blue, under-parts (often rufous) buff, streaked with
black, tail with broad black band. Female
(about Kestrel-size) has dark (not reddish)
brown upper-parts. (See illustration: black:
male Merlin, white: male Kestrel).

Nest usually on ground among heather; 4-5 eggs; May/June. Incubation by both sexes (28-32 days). Male brings food that female distributes
to young. These fly when about 4 w. old. Single-brooded.

Resident. Except for S. and E. England and Midlands breeding in
moorlands all over the country in small numbers. In autumn immigrants
on E. coast (Aug./Nov.).

*10-13 in.

*Lat. Falco columbarius / N. Am. Pigeon Hawk / D. Smelleken / F. Faucon
émerillon / G. Merlin / S. Dvärgfalk*

KESTREL

No other bird of prey of the falcon-type hovers so often and persistently as the Kestrel. (33-35 cm*) Male: chestnut upper-parts, head and tail bluish-grey, last with black band. Female: somewhat duller coloured, tail with several small bands.

Nest on ledges of cliffs, on buildings and in trees (often in old nests of other birds); 4-5 eggs; Apr./May. Incubation mainly by female (27-29 d.), tending of young by both parents. Young fly when about 4 w. old. Single-brooded.

Commonest bird of prey, breeding even in inner-London. Resident throughout the British Isles, except for the Shetlands, where only summer visitor.

*13-14 in.

Lat. Falco tinnunculus | N. Am. European Kestrel | D. Torenvalk | F. Faucon crécerelle | G. Turmfalke | S. Tornfalk

KESTREL

An impression of the flight action

Family ACCIPITRIDAE

OSPREY

Also known as Fish-Hawk. Brown above, white underparts and white head, with brown streaks on neck and breast. Soars and hovers above water; dives and seizes fish with its talons.

Rare migrant on east side of Great Britain, especially to Norfolk Broads and Scotland. In recent years has bred in Scotland again.

Latin. Pandion haliaetus / D. Vischarend / F. Balbuzard / G. Fischadler / S. Fiskgjuse

WHITE-TAILED EAGLE

Also known as Sea Eagle (90 cm*) this immense bird differs from golden eagle in that it develops a white tail at six years. Wing span 2.40 m** Female slightly taller. Brown plumage, head is paler shade.

Rare visitor to east coast and no longer breeds in British Isles.

*36 in. **8 ft.

Latin. Haliaetus albicilla / D. Zeearend / G. Seeadler / F. Pygargue ordinaire / S. Havsorn

GOLDEN EAGLE

The king of birds (80 cm*) is dark brown with golden head and neck Female is 7½ cm** longer than male. Has magnificent flight action.

Nest of sticks on crags; eggs 2; April.

Resident in north Scotland and the Western Isles where it also breeds.

*32 in. / **3 in.

Latin. Aquila chrysaëtos / *D. Steenarend* / *F. Aigle doré (or royal)* / *G. Steinadler* / *S. Kungsörn*

ROUGH-LEGGED BUZZARD

Main differences between Common Buzzard, which it closely resembles, are the feathered legs and the lighter head and breast. Brown above and light coloured underneath, it has long broad rounded wings and frequently hovers.

Winter visitor to East Coast of Britain, penetrating inland to the high ground of wild areas.

Latin. Buteo lagopus | D. Ruigpootbuizerd | F. Buse pattue | G. Rauhfussbussard | S. Fjällvråk

Wild Duck in flight formation

90

NOTES

The order Anseriformes comprises the wild fowl which of course can only be observed on or by water. Again the use of field glasses or a telescope is a necessity, for these are some of the most difficult birds to approach.

The geese can only be studied in Britain in the autumn and winter months when they come south to their feeding grounds from northern regions. These are only to be found in certain favoured districts, such as the flats of the east coast, the River Severn, estuaries and water land. A visit to these areas will give the bird watcher the opportunities of studying the birds or a sanctuary offers special facilities.

One of the most thrilling sights a bird watcher can experience is a long line of geese in the sky flying down from the north to their winter grounds. They come in, flying due south in one line after another and it is necessary to be on their line of flight in the North of England or Scotland to see them.

The ducks have considerable attraction and have been popularised through their ornamental use on public lakes in London and the provinces. Many such lakes have a wide selection of ducks which become surprisingly tame. These conditions offer opportunities for the watcher to approach the birds closely and in this way it is possible to familiarise oneself with the different species. Observing these birds in the field, however, is another matter and it means using one's opportunities when they present themselves. Several species breed in the north and come south or to inland areas as winter visitors. In some localities it is only in exceptionally severe weather that such birds are to be seen and it is necessary to be aware of all these factors. For example, during the most severe winter of this century, Smew, Pintail and other species visited a lake near London where they had not been seen before and neither have they been since; so weather can be a big factor in bird watching. One of the best

Wild Geese in flight formation

places of all is the coast of East Anglia and the Norfolk Broads where there is the richest of wild fowl life and in addition to species of duck and goose, the mighty wild Whooper Swans fly in over the sea in wedge formation from their breeding grounds in Northern lands. On this point of studying swans a visit to the famous Swannery at Abbotsbury in Dorset is recommended. This has been in existence for centuries and large numbers of swans breed and live here because the conditions of water and feeding are just right for them.

Hawks and Falcons are mostly seen on the wing. A familiar sight is the Kestrel hovering in the air watching the ground and suddenly swooping to its prey. The Kestrel may be seen in town as well as country and for this reason is the best known of all our hawks.

The Sparrow Hawk imposes itself on our notice by its lightning flight along the side of a hedge or a wood for the purpose of catching prey. A Sparrow Hawk flying at great speed along a hedgerow is one of the sights of the countryside.

The Buzzard with its big wings can be seen patiently hovering in the air in those districts it frequents, the south-west and west of Britain. The Harriers are more rare and are only likely to be spotted in those areas mentioned.

The Lord of the skies is the Peregrine Falcon the powerful bird which through the centuries has been trained and used for falconry. It is mainly found in mountainous districts and on sea cliffs. Only by watching the Peregrine Falcon tumbling across the skies can we appreciate its mastery of manoeuvre. It is a great experience to watch Peregrines playfully engaging in mock battles in the sky. Their movement in stooping and side-slipping is so fast that it is impossible to keep glasses focused on them.

Male Kestrel hovering

Mute Swan on nest

3

WADERS, SKUAS, GULLS, TERNS AND AUKS

Waders at the water's edge - Redshank; Oyster-catcher (in flight);
Curlew; Ringed Plover; Dunlin

3

CHARADRIIFORMES

FAMILIES REPRESENTED
IN PART 3

Charadriidae	Plovers
Haematopodidae	Oystercatcher
Scolopacidae	Sandpipers
Recurvirostridae	Avocet
Phalaropodidae	Phalaropes
Stercorariidae	Skuas
Laridae	Gulls, Terns
Alcidae	Auks

WADERS, SKUAS, GULLS,
TERNS AND AUKS

The Charadriiformes are a very big Order, comprising such birds as Plovers, Snipes, Sandpipers, Gulls, Terns, and even Guillemots and Puffin. Here interrelation is not so obvious, but running through each of the families of this order there is an unmistakable likeness. Everyone knows the Lapwing, which is a typical Plover (Charadriidae), and the Woodcock which is a typical Snipe (Scolopacidae) and has much in common with the Sandpipers, also belonging to the Scolopacidae.

The Skuas (Stercorariidae) have much in common with the Gulls (Laridae) and most of the Terns (also belonging to the Laridae), though much slenderer than the gulls, have the same brilliant white plumage.

Many of the Charadriiformes are to be found along our coasts, on mud-lands and estuaries, stretches of sand and shingle, where they can be seen in a great variety and considerable numbers.

Finally, this book deals with the interesting members of the Auk family (Alcidae).

GREENSHANK

Slightly bigger (30 cm*) than Redshank but
paler, with slightly upturned grey-blue bill
and long greenish legs. No white on wings.
Lower back, rump and tail white. Sexes alike.

Nest on the ground; 4 eggs; May/June. Incu-
bation (23-25 d.) and tending of young (leave nest; fly when about 4 w.
old) by both sexes. Single-brooded.

Summer-visitor, breeding in Scottish Highlands and Skye; elsewhere
common passage-migrant along British coasts, where some winter.

Lat. Tringa nebularia / D. Groenpootruiter / F. Chevalier aboyeur / G. Grün-
schenkel / S. Gluttsnäppa

*12 in.

PURPLE SANDPIPER

Small (21 cm*) dark wader with dark brownish bill, short yellow legs
and white wing-bar. Often to be found on rocks in company of Turn-
stones. Sexes alike.

Common passage-migrant and winter-visitor on all British coasts where
rocks offer suitable habitat. Only absent from early June to mid-July,
though some occasionally summer in the Shetlands.

*8½ in.

Lat. Calidris maritima / D. Paarse strandloper
F. Bécasseau maritime / G. Seestrandläufer /
S. Skärsnäppa

Order CHARADRIIFORMES   *Family CHARADRIIDAE*

RINGED PLOVER

Small (18 cm*) plover, colour-scheme somewhat similar to that of Lapwing, but upperparts are sandy-brown; black collar across chest. Narrow white wing-bar. (Short) bill orange with black tip; legs orange-yellow. Sexes alike. (See also page 143.)

Nest little hollow in ground; 4 eggs; May/June. Both sexes incubate (24-25 d.) and tend young (that leave nest). Double-brooded.

Summer visitor on British coasts, breeding widely inland; passage-migrants from N. Europe, some of which winter on sewage-farms and reservoirs.   *7½ in.

Lat. Charadrius hiaticula | N. Am. Semipalmated Plover | D. Bontbek-plevier | F. Grand gravelot | G. Sandregenpfeifer | S. Större strandpipare

LITTLE RINGED PLOVER (Char. dubius) is smaller (15 cm*), without white wing-bar, with flesh-coloured legs and yellow ring round eye; until about 1938 very rare vagrant, now summer-visitor, extending its range.   *6 in.

GREY PLOVER

Same size and closely resembling Golden Plover, but at all seasons and ages recognisable by black "arm pits" (only in flight), light rump and tail and light wing-bar. Sexes alike. Gregarious in winter.

Summer

The Grey Plover is a winter visitor and passage-migrant (Aug./May) while few may summer. Especially to be found along E. and S. coast of England, less common along W. coast and in Scotland; in Ireland scarce on S. coast.

Lat. Charadrius squatarola | N. Am. Black-bellied Plover | D. Zilverplevier | F. Pluvier argenté | G. Kiebitzregenpfeifer | S. Kustpipare

WOOD-SANDPIPER

Smaller (20 cm*) than Green Sandpiper. Long legs greenish, bill blackish. Rump white though less conspicuous than Green Sandpiper's. Tail barred. Under-side of wings light greyish. No wing-bar. Tends to be more gregarious and above all more noisy than Green Sandpiper.

Passage-migrant from mid-April to begin of June along E. and SE. coast of England, being rare on W. coast and very rare in Ireland.

*8 in.

Lat. Tringa glareola | D. Bosruiter | F. Chevalier sylvain | G. Bruchwasserläufer | S. Grönbena

TURNSTONE

This small wader has a striking pied appearance both in flight and when standing. It has a shortish bill, orange legs and in summer the upper parts have a colourful tortoiseshell appearance and the head is lighter coloured. It has a black band under the throat. In winter the upper parts are a darker brown.
It gets its name from the habit of turning over stones and weed in search of food.

Winter visitor; arrives on the East Coast in large flocks and is often found in company of other small waders. Some non-breeders stay on through the summer.

Latin. Arenaria interpres | D. Steenlooper | F. Tourne-pierre | G. Steinwalzer | S. Roskarl

OYSTER-CATCHER

Black (above) and white (under-parts) bird (42 cm*) with long orange-red bill and long pink legs. Winter: white half-collar on throat. Noisy bird when alarmed. Sexes alike. Large flocks outside breeding-season.

Nest shallow depression; 3 eggs; May. Incubation by both sexes (25-28 d.); young, which leave nest within few hours, are tended by both parents. Single-brooded.

Common breeding-bird along British coasts (rather scarce on E. and S. coast of England); in N. England, Scotland and some parts of E. Ireland often far inland. Wintering birds confined to the coasts.

*17 in.

Lat. Haematopus ostralegus | D. Scholekster | F. Huitrier pie | G. Austern-fischer | S. Strandskata

LAPWING

Relatively large (30 cm*) plover, black (metallic green) upper-parts and white rump; broad black band on chest; obvious black crest; tail white with black terminal band. In flight broad rounded wings are distinctive. Sexes almost alike. Forms large flocks outside breeding-season.

Nest shallow depression scraped by male and female; 4 eggs; Apr./May. Incubation by both sexes (24-27 d.). Young stay at least 24 h. in nest; they are tended mainly by female. Single-brooded.

Common resident throughout Britain. British birds partially migrate and are replaced in autumn by large flocks from the Continent.

*12 in.

Lat. Vanellus vanellus / Also: Peewit / D. Kievit / F. Vanneau huppé / G. Kiebitz / S. Tofsvipa

GOLDEN PLOVER

About Lapwing-size (28 cm*). Upper-parts in summer gold and black spangled, face, cheeks and rump black; northern race (*altifrons*) with conspicuous white band seaming black of rump; in southern race (*apricarius*) this pattern is far less clear cut, the white band being often even absent. Sexes alike. Gregarious in winter.

Nest shallow depression; 4 (3) eggs; Apr./May. Incubation (27-28 d.) and tending of young by both sexes. Young fly when 4 w. old. Single-brooded.

Southern race breeds in N. England and N. Wales, Scotland and Ireland. In winter migrants belonging to northern race mix with our Golden Plovers. The races then cannot be told apart and even in summer this is very difficult because of intermediates.

*11 in.

Lat. Charadrius apricarius | D. Goudplevier | F. Pluvier doré | G. Goldregenpfeifer | S. Ljungpipare

107

KENTISH PLOVER

Often confused with Ringed Plover, but is somewhat smaller (15 cm*) and has interrupted collar; lead-grey legs and bill. Female has no black on fore-head and brown (interrupted) collar. More gregarious than Ringed Plover.

Nest little hollow; 3-4 eggs; May/June. Incubation (24 d.) and managing of young (that leave nest) by both parents. Single- (double-) brooded.

Only breeding-populations in Kent and occasionally Sussex. Rare passage-migrant, most often in autumn along E. and S.E. coast of England.

*6 in.

Lat. Charadrius alexandrinus | D. Strandplevier | F. Gravelot à collier inter-rompu | G. Seeregenpfeifer | S. Svartbent strandpipare

CURLEW

Large (50-60 cm*) wader with very long (12 cm**) strongly curved bill, larger than Whimbrel (38-40 cm***), which has shorter bill (8 cm****), though dimensions are only conclusive when the two species are seen together, especially as young Curlews have much shorter bills than adult birds. Sexes alike.

Nest shallow depression; 4 eggs; Apr./May. Incubation (28-30 d.) and managing of young by both sexes. Young fly when 5-6 w. old. Single-brooded.

Resident, breeding commonly throughout Britain, though very local in S. and E. England and Midlands. After breeding-season most birds move to the coast, where joined by winter visitors from the Continent.

Lat. Numenius arquata | D. Wulp | F. Courlis cendré | G. Grosser Brachvogel | S. Storspov

THE WHIMBREL *(Numenius phaeopus)* breeds in the Shetlands and few other places. Passage-migrants (Apr./June and July/Oct.) occur on all coasts of Britain.

*20-24 in. **5 in. ***15-16 in. ****3½ in.

BLACK-TAILED GODWIT

Rather large (38-40 cm*), long legs, bill (10 cm**) and neck. In summer chestnut colour of head, neck and chest is quite characteristic of this species. Broad white wing-bars and white tail with broad black terminal band make Black-tailed easily recognisable.

Passage-migrant especially on E. and S. coasts of England. Breeding in increasing numbers in E. England.

BAR-TAILED GODWIT slightly smaller.

*15-17 in. **4 in.

Lat. Limosa limosa | D. Grutto | F. Barge à queue noire | G. Uferschnepfe | S. Rödspov

Tails of:

Black-tailed
Godwit

Bar-tailed
Godwit

GREEN SANDPIPER

About Thrush-size (22 cm*). Under-side of wings blackish, rump and tail pure white contrasting to near-black upper-parts. Whitish eye-stripe; no wing-bar. Legs greenish, straight bill blackish. Sexes alike. To be found along margins of fresh waters of all kinds (even small pools), rarely on the open shore. Has habit of sudden dashing from hidden, spots with shrill call.

Passage-migrants (July/Nov. and Mch/May), common throughout the British Isles though rather rare in Scotland (except E. parts) and irregular in Ireland. Breeding in Westmorland was proved in 1917 and summering birds have been observed elsewhere.

*9 in.

Lat. Tringa ochropus | D. Witgatje | F. Chevalier cul-blanc | G. Waldwasser-läufer | S. Skogssnäppa

Order CHARADRIIFORMES

Family SCOLOPACIDAE

RUFF

Male in summer-plumage with obvious ruff and ear-tufts of varying colour. Female and male in winter-plumage very much like Redshank, but having shorter legs and also, shorter bills. At all seasons tail black with conspicuous white patch at each side. Male 28-30 cm*; female (Reeve) 23-25 cm**.

Passage-migrant from March to October (though seldom between

*11-12 in. **9-10 in.

mid-June and mid-July), more frequent in autumn (especially young birds) than in spring. Fairly often inland. Has bred recently in Norfolk and once regularly in other parts.

Lat. Philomachus pugnax | D. Kemphaantje | F. Chevalier combattant | G. Kampfläufer | S. Brushane

KNOT

Rather small (25 cm*) stocky bird with straight black bill and short olive-green legs. In summer under-parts rufous, in winter grey and white. Tail uniform grey. Sexes alike. Highly gregarious, feeding in densely packed masses along sandy and muddy shores.

Passage-migrant and winter visitor especially to E. coast and on W. coast from Solway to Dee (Cheshire). Uncommon inland.

*10 in.

Lat. Calidris canutus / *D.* Kanoetstrandloper / *F.* Bécasseau maubèche / *G.* Knutt / *S.* Kustsnäppa

REDSHANK

Much bigger (28 cm*) than former species; long orange-red legs; bill red at base. Rump and conspicuous patch along hind-border of wing white. Tail barred. Sexes alike.

Well-concealed nest in tufts of grass; 4 eggs; Apr./May. Incubation (22-24 d.) and tending of young (leave nest; fly when about 4 w. old) by both parents. Single-brooded.

Partly resident (though many breeding-birds migrate to Ireland or France) breeding all over the British Isles (except Cornwall, Pembroke and S. Ireland). Breeding-birds from the Continent and Iceland winter in Britain.

*11 in.

Lat. Tringa totanus | D. Tureluur | F. Chevalier gambette | G. Rotschenkel | S. Rödbena

COMMON SANDPIPER

Small (19 cm*) with short dark-brown bill and short greenish legs. Obvious white wing-bar. Back, rump and tail grey-brown, the last with white margin. Sexes alike.

Nest on ground often close to water; 4 eggs; May/June. Incubation (21-22 d.) and tending of young by both parents. Single-brooded.

Summer visitor (Apr./Oct.) breeding in hilly districts of Scotland, Wales, N. and W. England (rare elsewhere) and Ireland (but for SE.).

*7½ in.

Lat. Tringa hypoleucos | D. Oeverloper | F. Chevalier guignette | G. Fluszufer-läufer | S. Drillsnäppa

DUNLIN

In summer this small (19 cm*) wader has black belly. In winter upper-
parts brownish-grey, breast greyish, not pure white. No blackish
shoulder-spot. Rather long blackish bill may be slightly curved.

Nest on the ground near water; 4 eggs; May/June. Incubation (3 w.)
and tending of young (leave nest; fly when about 3 w. old) by both
parents.

Breeds in Hebrides, Orkneys and Shetlands, Scottish mainland and
(sparingly) in N. parts of England. Breeding birds belong to S. race
C.a. schinzii, while C.a. alpina (not separable in the field) which breeds
in arctic Europe and W. Siberia passes along our coasts and winters in
very great numbers.

*7½ in.

*Lat. Calidris alpina | N. Am. Red-backed Sandpiper | D. Bonte strandloper |
F. Bécasseau variable | G. Alpenstrandläufer | S. Kärrsnäppa*

SANDERLING

Rather plump bird (20 cm*) with short straight black bill and short black legs. Very light appearance in winter, under-parts and most of the head being white. Dark spot at shoulder. White wing-bar. Sexes alike. Gregarious, with distinct preference for sandy shores where extremely restless while feeding in small flocks.

Passage-migrant and winter visitor to all suitable (sandy) coasts of Britain, rather scarce in NW. and N. of Scotland. Uncommon inland. Non-breeding birds are often observed in summertime, though the species breeds only in arctic Europe, Asia and America.

*8 in.

Lat. Crocethia alba | D. Drieteentje | F. Bécasseau sanderling | G. Sanderling | S. Sandlöpare

118

AVOCET

Snow-white bird (43 cm*) with black streaks and patches, long greenish-grey legs and strikingly upcurved black bill. Sexes alike.

Social breeder; 4 (5) eggs; May. Incubation (22-24 d.) and tending of young (leave nest; fly when about 6 w. old) by both parents. Single-brooded.

Has been extinct as breeding-bird but has nested in Ireland (1938), Norfolk (1941) and since 1947 in Suffolk, in small numbers. Otherwise scarce migrant.

*17 in.

Lat. Recurvirostra avosetta / D. Kluut / F. Avocette / G. Säbelschnäbler /
S. Skärfläcka

RED-NECKED PHALAROPE

Small (17 cm*) wader, often seen swimming (very buoyant). Very slender black bill. In summer: white throat and under-parts, rufous-red patch on sides of neck. In winter: grey back streaked white.

Social breeder near water; 4 eggs; May/June. Incubation (20-21 d.) and tending of young (leave nest; fly when about 3 w. old) by male only. Single-brooded.

Summer visitor (May-Aug.) breeding in small numbers in Orkneys, Shetland, O. Hebrides and few spots in NW. Ireland. Otherwise scarce passage-migrant, most often on S. and E. coasts of England.

*6½ in.

Lat. Phalaropus lobatus | N. Am. Northern Phalarope | D. Grauwe franjepoot | F. Phalarope à bec grêle | G. Odinshühnchen | S. Smalnäbbad simsnäppa

Order CHARADRIIFORMES   *Family PHALAROPODIDAE*

GREY PHALAROPE

Slightly bigger (20 cm*) than Red-necked. Somewhat stouter bill yellow at base, legs yellowish. In summer: chestnut under-parts and throat. In winter much like Red-necked, under-parts being white. Grey back more uniform coloured (without whitish streaks), lighter than wings. Shape (yellow with black tip) and colour (shorter and thicker) of bill are best field-marks.

In contrast to most other species female phalaropes are brighter coloured than males. They take a leading part in courtship and leave incubation and tending of young to the males. Usually phalaropes are extremely tame which allows close approach needed to tell the two species apart.

Scarce passage-migrant (Sept./Dec.) along SW., S. and E. coast of England, very scarce elsewhere and at other seasons.

*8 in.

Lat. Phalaropus fulicarius | N. Am. Red Phalarope | D. Rosse franjepoot | F. Phalarope à bec large | G. Thorshühnchen | S. Brednäbbad simsnäppa

ARCTIC SKUA

Slender dark gull-like bird, about size of Black-headed (35-37 cm*) with long projecting central tail-feathers (5-7 cm**). Uniform dark brown phases are known as well as light ones with white under-parts and many intermediates. Dark phase is commonest in Britain. The Arctic Skua has the habit (as have other skuas) of pursuing terns and small gulls until these drop the fish they are carrying or even disgorge their last meal. The small skuas (of which the Arctic Skua is commonest in Britain) are very similar while still immature. Sexes alike.

Summer visitor and passage-migrant to E. and S. coast of England, less to W. coast and Ireland. Breeds in Shetlands and (less) on Fair Isle, Orkneys, I. and O. Hebrides, Caithness and Sutherland.

*35-37 in. **2-3½ in.

Lat. Stercorarius parasiticus | N. Am. Parasitic Jaeger | D. Kleine jager | F. Labbe parasite | G. Schmarotzerraubmöwe | S. Vannlig labb

122

GREAT SKUA

About size (and rather much like) immature Herring Gull, with conspicuous white patch on wings, shorter, thicker black bill, shorter tail and blackish legs. Length about 58 cm*. Sexes alike. Chases gulls and terns for food but may also be seen fishing for itself.

Summer visitor (Apr./Sept.) breeding in the Orkneys and Shetlands, very rare in Ireland.

Lat. Stercorarius skua | N. Am. Skua | D. Grote jager | F. Grand Labbe | G. Grosse Raubmöwe | S. Storlabb   *23 in.

POMARINE SKUA

About the size of common Gull (43-45 cm*), otherwise very much like Arctic Skua of which adult birds may be told by broad, blunt and twisted central tail-feathers projecting 5-7½ cm** from tail. It has dark and light phases and intermediates. Chases terns and gulls for food like other skuas.

Rather regular autumn visitor (Aug./Nov.) to E. and S. coasts of England, scarce to rare at other coasts and other seasons.

Lat. Stercorarius pomarinus | N. Am. Pomarine Jaeger | D. Middelste jager | F. Labbe pomarin | G. Mittlere Raubmöwe | S. Bredstjärtad labb   *17-18 in. **2-3 in.

LONG-TAILED SKUA

Slightly smaller (33-35 cm*) than Arctic Skua with very long (12-20 cm**) central tail-feathers, but beware of confusion with light-coloured Arctic Skua with very long tail-feathers. Immature birds are still more confusing. (Illus. p. 142.)

Scarce and irregular autumn visitor (Aug./Oct.), mainly to E. coast of England.

Lat. Stercorarius longicaudus | N. Am. Long-tailed Jaeger | D. Kleinste jager | F. Labbe longicaude | G. Kleine Raubmöwe | S. Fjällabb

123

*13-14 in. **5-8 in.

GREAT BLACK-BACKED GULL

Big (63-68 cm*) black-mantled gull with flesh-coloured to whitish (never yellow) legs. Immature birds very much like young Herring-Gulls but head and under-parts at all ages somewhat lighter. Sexes alike.

Social (not always) breeder on rocky coasts and islands; 3 eggs; May/June. Incubation (26-28 d.) and managing of young (fly when 7-8 w.) by both sexes. Single-brooded.

Resident, breeding locally along British coasts, though scarce on E. coast of England and in Scotland south of Moray Firth. In autumn and winter widespread on all coasts.

*25-27 in.

Lat. Larus marinus | D. Grote mantelmeeuw | F. Goéland marin | G. Mantelmöwe | S. Havstrut

LESSER BLACK-BACKED GULL

Smaller (53 cm*) edition of Great Black-back (though size is never conclusive) with yellow legs. In winter even the colour of the legs of adult birds resemble that of Herring Gull's and immature birds of both species are all but undistinguishable. Lesser Black-backs breeding in Britain belong to the race L. f. graelsii (Faroes, British Isles, Channel Islands and Brittany) and have rather pale mantle (always lighter than black wing-tips), varying from nearly slate-grey to nearly the silver-grey of Herring Gull's. In L. f. fuscus (Scandinavia, the Baltic and N. Russia) the colour of the mantle is same as Great Black-back's. Beware of intermediates and cross-breds with Herring Gull. Sexes alike.

Social breeder on rocky coasts and islands; 3 eggs; May/June. Incubation (26-28 d.) by both sexes, but only female tends young that fly when about 5 w. Single-brooded.

The British race is a summer visitor (Febr./Nov.) breeding commonly in Wales, N. England, Scotland and Ireland and (less numerous) on S. and SW. coasts of England. The Scandinavian race (L. f. fuscus) visits the E. coast of England in autumn and winter.

*21 in.

Lat. Larus fuscus | D. Kleine mantelmeeuw | F. Goéland brun | G. Heringsmöwe | S. Sillmås

HERRING-GULL

Commonest of British gulls, bigger (50-60 cm*) than Mew Gull, with heavy yellow bill (red spot near tip), flesh-coloured legs and pale lemon-coloured eyes. The immatures of Great Black-back, Lesser Black-back, Herring-Gull, and Mew Gull are very difficult (often impossible to tell apart. Sexes alike.

Social breeder on rocky coasts and islands; 3 eggs; May/June. Incubation (25-27 ins.) and tending of young (fly when 5-6 w. old) by both sexes. Single-brooded.

Common resident, whose numbers are greatly augmented by winter visitors and passage-migrants from NW. Europe.

*20-24 in.

Lat. Larus argentatus / D. Zilvermeeuw / F. Goéland argenté / G. Silbermöwe / S. Gråtrut

BLACK TERN

Small (22-25 cm*) dark tern with only slightly forked tail, black bill and near-black red-brown feet. No white on slate-grey upper-parts; no white fore-wing. Immature birds and adults in winter-plumage can be very confusing. Sexes alike.

Rather irregular passage-migrant in spring (Apr./June) and autumn (July/Oct.) along E. and S. coasts of England. Some may be seen inland. Has bred in E. England till middle of 19th century and recently in E. England.

*9-10 in.

Lat. Chlidonias niger | D. Zwarte stern | F. Guifette noire | G. Trauerseeschwalbe | S. Svarttärna

COMMON TERN (above)

Order *CHARADRIIFORMES*
Family *LARIDAE*

Elegant white bird (32-35 cm* including deeply forked tail) with silver-gray wings and back, black crown and nape. Red legs and vermilion-red black-tipped bill. Sexes alike. In winter-plumage this and following species are very difficult if not impossible to tell from each other. Social breeder; 2-3 eggs; May/June. Incubation (21-28 d.) and tending of young (fly when about 4 w. old) by both parents. Single-brooded. Summer visitor (Apr./Oct.), breeding along all suitable coasts of the British Isles (except S. Wales) and sometimes inland in Scotland and Ireland.

Lat. Sterna hirundo / D. Visdiefje / F. Sterne pierregarin / G. Fluszseeschwalbe
/ S. Fisktärna

*13-14 in.

ARCTIC TERN

Closely resembling Common Tern but blood-red bill (adults in summer) has no black tip and legs are distinctly shorter. Length 35-38 cm*, owing to greater length of tail. Social breeder (often associates with Common Tern); 2 eggs; May/June. Both sexes incubate (21-22 d.) and tend young that fly when 3-4 weeks old. Single-brooded.

Summer visitor and passage-migrant (Apr./Oct.), breeding in England only along NW. coast and on Farne Is., in Wales off Anglesey, in Scotland and Ireland on all coasts.

Lat. Sterna macrura | D. Noordse stern | F. Sterne arctic | G. Küstenseeschwalbe | S. Rödnäbbad tärna

*14-15 in.

ROSEATE TERN

Closely resembling Common Tern as well as Arctic Tern but in summer adult Roseate Terns can be told from these by black colour of bill (legs red). Juveniles and young birds are very tricky. Sexes alike.

Scarce summer visitor and passage-migrant (May/Sept.), a few pairs breeding on coasts of Dorset and Norfolk and on Farne Is., also in NW. England and (recently) in the Scilly Is. Some colonies in Wales, on E. coast of Scotland and in Ireland.

Lat. Sterna dougallii | D. Dougalls stern | F. Sterne de Dougall | G. Paradiesseeschwalbe | S. Dougalls tärna

129

BLACK-HEADED GULL

This small slender gull (35-38 cm*) is easily recognised at all ages and seasons by broad white margin to front of black-tipped wings. Adults have red bill and legs. In summer (Mch/Sept.) chocolate-brown hood. Sexes alike.

Social breeder along coasts as well as inland; 3 eggs; Apr./June. Incubation (22-24 d.) and managing of young (fly when 4-5 w. old) by both parents. Single-brooded.

Resident (though some breeding-birds may winter in Spain or even N. Africa) breeding in varying numbers along all British coasts and in some inland colonies. Winter visitors and passage-migrants from W. and NW. Europe.

*14-15 in.

Lat. Larus ridibundus | D. Kokmeeuw | F. Mouette rieuse | G. Lachmöwe | S. Skrattmås

COMMON GULL

Slender yellow-green bill (no red spot) and legs, black wing-tips with white spots and dark-brown eyes distinguish adults (40 cm*) from other Gulls. Immature Common Gulls are difficult to tell from other species though more or less dark subterminal band on tail may be of help. Sexes alike.

Social breeder (no large colonies) along the coasts; 3 eggs; May/June. Incubation (22-25 d.) and tending of young (fly when 4-5 w. old) by both parents. Single-brooded.

Resident, breeding commonly only in Scotland and at Dungeness; irregularly in Cumberland. W. coast of Ireland. Otherwise a winter visitor from NW. Europe to all coasts as well as inland.

Lat. Larus canus / Also: Mew Gull / D. Stormmeeuw / F. Goeland cendré / G. Sturmmöwe / S. Fiskmås

*16 in.

Above: Kittiwake
Below: Common Gull

KITTIWAKE

Same size (40 cm*) but slenderer than Common Gull with black-tipped (no white spots) wings and black legs. Yellow bill and dark eyes. Mantle a shade darker than Common Gull's. Sexes alike.

Social breeder on cliff-ledges; 2 eggs; May/June. Incubation (21-28 d.) and tending of young by both parents. Single-brooded.

Breeds very locally along NE., NW. and SW. coasts of England and along coast of Wales. Locally along coast of Scotland and rather abundantly along Irish coasts. Really abundantly on Orkneys, Shetlands and Hebrides. Common offshore in winter when heavy storms may sweep stray birds inland. In autumn Kittiwakes disperse from breeding colonies in S. and W. directions, ringed birds having been recovered off E. coast of N. America.

Colour picture page 131

*16 in.

Lat. Rissa tridactyla / *D. Drieteenmeeuw* / *F. Mouette tridactyle* / *G. Drei-zehenmöwe* / *S. Tretåig mås*

SANDWICH TERN

Largest of more common terns (38-42 cm*), somewhat heavier with less deeply forked tail. Black bill with pale-yellow tip and black feet. Sexes alike.

Social breeder (often in large colonies); 2 (3) eggs; May/June. Incubation (21-24 d.) and tending of young (fly when 5 w. old) by both parents. Single-brooded.

Summer visitor and passage-migrant (Apr./Oct.). Breeds in England in Farne Is., N. Norfolk and NW. England; in Wales on Anglesey only; in Scotland on coasts of mainland and some islands; in Ireland mainly in N. and W. (also inland). Otherwise passage-migrant from the Continent.

*15-17 in.

Lat. Sterna sandvicensis | N. Am. Cabot's Tern | D. Grote stern | F. Sterne caujek | G. Brandseeschwalbe | S. Kentsk tärna

LITTLE TERN

Very small (22-25 cm*, tail included) with yellow black-tipped bill, yellow legs and white forehead (Other Terns also have white foreheads in winter plumage). Sexes alike.

Social breeder (small colonies); 2-3 eggs; May/June. Both sexes incubate (19-21 d.) and tend young that fly when 4 w. old. Single-brooded.

Summer visitor (Apr./Sept.) breeding on all coasts of England and Wales (except Cornwall and S. Wales) and some parts of Scotland (also Hebrides and probably Orkneys); in Ireland only on E. coast. Otherwise passage-migrant strictly confined to the coasts.

*9-10 in.

Lat. Sterna albifrons | D. Dwergstern | F. Sterne naine | G. Zwergseeschwalbe | S. Småtärna

GUILLEMOT

Black and white like Razorbill but with straight pointed bill. In summer head and neck are dark without any white. In winter face and neck are white with conspicuous dark streak behind the eye. Length 40-42 cm*. Sexes alike.

Social breeder on cliff-ledges; 1 egg; May/June. Incubation (4-5 w.) and tending of young by both sexes. Single-brooded.

Resident, breeding in same localities as Razorbill and often together with this species. From Scotland northwards the dark northern U.a. aalge breeds; south of Berwick and Argyll is U.a. albionis which is somewhat lighter.

(See also page 144.)

*16-17 in.

Lat. Uria aalge | D. Zeekoet | F. Guillemot de troïl | G. Trottellumme | S. Sillgrissla

RAZORBILL

This black and white sea-bird (40 cm*) is easily recognisable by its unique bill. In summer head and neck are black with a small white line from base of bill to the eye. In winter throat and sides of neck are white. Juveniles have smaller bills. Sexes alike. (See page 144.)

Social breeder on cliff-ledges; 1 egg; May/June. Both sexes incubate (33-36 d.) and tend young that flutters down to sea when about 2 w. old, where it is fed by one of the parents. Single-brooded.

Resident, breeding on all suitable coasts of the British Isles (except E. coast between Isle of Wight and Yorkshire.)

*16 in.

Lat. Alca torda | D. Alk | F. Pingouin torda | G. Tordalk | S. Tordmule

BLACK GUILLEMOT

Smaller (33-35 cm*) than Guillemot; adult birds in summer plumage are all-black except for large white patch on wing. Bill black, legs red. In winter upper parts barred black and white, head and under-parts white. Sexes alike.

Social breeder (small numbers) in hollows; 2 eggs; May/June. Both sexes incubate (28-34 d.) and tend young that fly when 5 w. old. Single-brooded.

Resident, breeding on coast of Cumberland, Isle of Man, N. and W. coasts and isles of Scotland and (locally) all around Ireland. Stay in breeding area in winter.

*13-14 in.

Summer

Winter

Lat. Uria grylle | D. Zwarte zeekoet | F. Guillemot à miroir | G. Gryllteiste | S. Tobisgrissla

Order CHARADRIIFORMES   *Family ALCIDAE*

PUFFIN

Small (30 cm*) clown-like black and white bird with brightly-coloured thickly shaped bill. Feet orange.

Social breeder in burrows; 1 egg; May. Both sexes incubate (40-42 d.) and tend young for about 40 d. It is then deserted and stays in nest for 7-10 d. when it flutters down to sea. Single-brooded.

Resident, breeding at same localities (but in fewer numbers) as Guillemot and Razorbill. On east coast of England in Farne Is. and Flamborough only. Specially favours islands off Welsh coast.

*12 in.

Lat. Fratercula arctica | N. Am. Atlantic Puffin | D. Papegaaiduiker | F. Macareux moine | G. Papageitaucher | S. Lunnefågel

NOTES

Birds of the Order CHARADRIIFORMES, which form the subject of pages 102 to 138, are to be found mainly along the coast, on mud flats and estuaries. The Lapwings however are inland nesting birds. All of these birds are of fairly large size and very attractive to study. It is also possible to approach within reasonable distance of many of them, an exception being some Plovers, which are very wary, no doubt through persecution.

If one can find the right place it is possible to see many of these birds in the same locality. The coasts of East Anglia, Scotland and Ireland are excellent areas for first hand study. Indeed, there is no telling what else the bird watcher may see particularly in East Anglia, for there are records of visits of vagrants from places as far away as Siberia, the Caspian Sea and the Mediterranean. He can lie in the sand hills and sweep the shore with a pair of glasses and observe without interruption.

Gulls are the most fascinating of birds for they are true world wanderers. It is only necessary to see them following a ship for hour after hour or day after day to realise they are at home anywhere and with their amazing strength of wing can be in the far north one week and on the Coast of France the next. It is a point to be able to separate the different kinds of gulls and then move on to the Terns with their wonderful flight into the wind skimming the water with all the grace of a swallow. There is no more lovely sea bird than a Tern on the wing and it is possible to be charmed by their action of flying and grace of movement. Not without reason are they called Sea Swallows.

Although the Skuas may visit the east coast in autumn they breed in the far north of Britain and a visit there is necessary to study their reproductive behaviour.

The Waders can hold our interest for hours on end. They are always so busy and full of activity and at the same time are both quaint and charming. The sea shore, mud flats, and the estuaries are their home ground.

The Razorbill, Guillemots and Puffin are mostly birds of the

Lapwing nestlings

Long-tailed Skua

West coast particularly the islands off the coast of Wales and the North West. Here bird sanctuaries are to be found where there are opportunities of closer study. The social breeding of the Auks is one of the outstanding features of interest in bird life.

Since 1947 the Avocet has been breeding in increasing numbers near Orford in Suffolk after having been extinct in Britain as a breeding bird for many years.

Ringed Plover

Above left: Guillemot in Summer plumage
Above right: Guillemot in Winter plumage
Below: Razorbill in Winter

4

DOVES TO CROWS

Rooks in flight

4

DOVES TO CROWS

Part four deals with eight orders; Columbiformes, Cuculiformes, Strigiformes, Apodiformes, Coraciiformes, Piciformes, Caprimulgiformes and part of the Passeriformes. The first six orders, which are comparatively small, are easily distinguishable because the birds belonging to them are all characteristic of their order and all have in common an unmistakable resemblance.

Columbiformes comprise Pigeons and Doves and this order is known and seen all over the country and in many towns and cities as well. The Cuckoo is the only member of the *Cuculiformes* that is commonly seen in Britain. It is best known for its song and you may arouse this bird's interest by imitating its call. This may also be done with other birds, though they may be less easy to imitate.

The *Strigiformes* are the Owls. With their big heads and staring eyes they have a distinctive appearance and a striking family likeness which makes them the easiest of birds to identify. Their nocturnal habits may be a handicap in studying them. However, the Little Owl and the Short-eared Owl may often be seen by day, and most of them start hunting while it is twilight.

The well-known Swift is the only representative of the *Apodiformes* in the British Isles and has only a superficial likeness to Swallows and Martins which belong to the big order of the *Passeriformes*. The Kingfisher is one of two representatives of the *Coraciiformes;* this flying streak of brilliant colour, though not commonly seen, is again an easy bird to recognize as is the Hoopoe, a rare but regular visitor. The Woodpeckers *(Piciformes)* are easy to identify and they proclaim their presence by loud drumming on branches and trunks of trees. The Green Woodpecker drums rather less, but it has a loud ringing "laugh" which can be heard at a considerable distance.

The Nightjar is a representative of the *Caprimulgiformes*. There remains the large order of the *Passeriformes* or Perching Birds which includes not only the song birds but also Swallows and Martins, Ravens and Crows. This book deals with the Larks, the Swallows and the Martins, the Golden Oriole, and the common members of the Crow family (Corvidae).

FAMILIES REPRESENTED
IN PART 4

Columbidae	Pigeons and Doves
Cuculidae	Cuckoo
Tytonidae	Barn-Owl
Strigidae	Owls
Caprimulgidae	Nightjar
Apodidae	Swift
Alcedinidae	Kingfisher
Upupidae	Hoopoe
Picidae	Woodpeckers
Alaudidae	Larks
Hirundinidae	Swallows and Martins
Oriolidae	Oriole
Corvidae	Crows
Certhiidae	Creeper

Order COLUMBIFORMES   *Family COLUMBIDAE*

ROCK-DOVE

Somewhat like Stock-Dove (32 cm*) but conspicuous white rump, two black wing-bars, no black wing-tips, no white on neck or wings. Sexes alike.

Nest in holes of cliffs or among rocks; 2 eggs; Apr./June. Incubation 17-18 d.) and tending of young (fly when about 5 w. old) by both sexes. Double-brooded (at least).

Resident, breeding in decreasing numbers along Scottish and Irish coasts (not S. of Firth of Forth).

*13 in.

Lat. Columba livia | D. Rotsduif | F. Pigeon biset | G. Felsentaube | S. Klippduva

STOCK-DOVE

Rather like domestic pigeon. Length about 32 cm*. No white on neck or wings. No white rump. Black-tipped wings. Irridescent green patch (not white) on sides of neck. Sexes alike.

Nest in holes of trees (even rabbit-burrows); 2 eggs; Mch/Sept. Incubation (16-18 d.) and tending of young (fly when about 4 w. old) by both parents. Double-brooded (at least).

Resident, breeding all over British Isles except N. Scotland), rather local in Ireland. Some of the young birds emigrate.

*13 in.

Lat. Columba oenas / D. Holenduif / F. Pigeon colombin / G. Hohltaube / S. Skogsduva

Order COLUMBI-
FORMES

Family COLUMBIDAE

WOOD-PIGEON

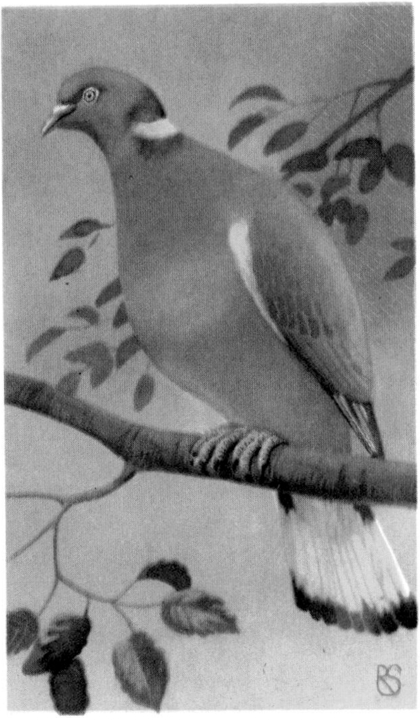

Large (40 cm*) blue-grey pigeon with broad white band across wing and white patch on sides of neck. Rather long tail. Immature birds lack white patch on the neck. Sexes alike.

Nest in trees, hedgerows and on buildings; 2 eggs; Mch/Oct. Incubation (17-20 d.) and tending of young (fly when 5 w. old) by both parents. Double-brooded.

Resident, breeding all over the British Isles (except Shetland, where passage-migrant) but scarce in N. Scotland.

*16 in.

Lat. Columba palumbus / D. Houtduif / F. Pigeon ramier / G. Ringeltaube / S. Ringduva

Order COLUMBIFORMES   *Family COLUMBIDAE*

TURTLE-DOVE

Distinctly smaller (27 cm*) than Wood-Pigeon with long white-tipped black tail. Upper-parts rufous-brown. Immature birds lack patch of black and white feathers on sides of neck. Sexes alike.

Nest in tall hedgerows and trees; 2 eggs; May/July. Incubation (13-14 d.) and tending of young (fly when about 3 w. old) by both parents. Double-brooded.

Summer visitor (April/May to Oct.) breeding in S. and E. England and Midlands, rare in Devon and Cornwall and W. Wales. Irregular passage-migrant to Scotland. Scarce visitor to S. Ireland.

*11 in.

Lat. Streptopelia turtur | D. Tortelduif | F. Tourterelle des bois | G. Turtel-taube | S. Turturduva

COLLARED DOVE

Distinguished by a black collar this dove has established itself in Britain since about 1955. Previously a rare bird it now breeds in many parts of the country. (28 cm*.) Sandy-grey plumage. Sexes alike, similar to Turtle Dove but is evenly coloured on the upper parts and has more white on the under-side of the tail. Juveniles darker than adults. Usually tame.

Nests in trees, tall shrubs and hedgerows. 2 eggs. March/July. Double-brooded (at least).

*11 in.

Lat. Streptopelia decaocto | D. Turksetortel | F. Tourterelle turque | G. Türkentaube | S. Skrattduva

LONDON PIGEON

The London Pigeon is similar to Stock-Dove, but occurs in differing plumage types. They may be blue rock, blue chequer, red rock, red chequer, black, white or any of those colours splashed with white. Gregarious and found in the centre of towns where they feed in the streets and squares; also in many seaside resorts and country districts. There is much crossing which accounts for the variety of plumage and domesticated or carrier pigeons joining wild or semi-wild flocks carry the admixture still further.

Order CUCULIFORMES   *Family CUCULIDAE*

CUCKOO

Slender bird (33 cm*) somewhat like male Sparrow-Hawk though pointed wings and long graduated white-tipped tail are characteristic, as is call-note. Sexes alike.

No nest as eggs (up to 15-20) are laid in nests of other species, especially small passerines, after removing one of the foster-parents' eggs. The young Cuckoo (which hatches out after 12-13 days) ejects eggs or young of foster-parents. It flies when about 4 w. old.

Summer visitor (Apr./Sept.) generally distributed all over the British Isles (except Shetland, where scarce migrant).
Occasionally south-coast end of March, generally Apr./Sept; adults leave August, young follow Sept. and Oct.

*13 in.

Lat. Cuculus canorus | D. Koekoek | F. Coucou gris | G. Kuckuck |S. Gök

BARN-OWL

Rather large (35 cm*) very pale owl. Heart-shaped face and under-parts white, upper-parts orange-buff. Sexes alike.

Nest in buildings or ruins and in holes of trees or cliffs; 4-7 eggs; Apr./May (Dec.). Incubation (32-34 d.) by female only; male assists in feeding of young which fly when 9-10 w. old. Single- (double-) brooded.

Resident breeding all over the British Isles except NE. Scotland.

*14 in.

Lat. Tyto alba | D. Kerkuil | F. Chouette effraye | G. Schleiereule | S. Tornuggla

Order STRIGIFORMES
Family STRIGIDAE

LITTLE OWL

Small (22 cm*) plump flat-headed owl, greyish-brown with white spots. Often seen by daylight, when mobbed by passerine birds. Likes perching on wires or telegraph-poles. Sexes alike.

Nest in holes of trees, walls, cliffs and even rabbit-burrows; 3-5 eggs; Apr./May. Incubation (28-30 d.) by hen only but male assists in feeding of young which fly when 5-7 w. old. Single-(double-) brooded.

Introduced (first 1842, later 1879 and 1896) from Italy. Now breeding in England and Wales (N. to Northumberland). Resident.

*9 in.

Lat. Athene noctua | D. Steenuil | F. Chouette chevêche | G. Steinkauz | S. Minervas uggla

159

Order STRIGIFORMES   Family STRIGIDAE

TAWNY OWL

Rather large (38 cm*) thick-headed short-winged owl with big black eyes. No ear-tufts. Mottled brown. Sexes alike.

Nest in holes of trees or in old nests of other birds; 2-4 eggs; Febr./Apr. Incubation (28-30 d.) by female only but male brings food to the young which fly when about 5 w. old. Single-brooded.

Resident breeding all over the British Isles (though uncommon in the W. and not in N. isles).

Lat. Strix aluco | D. Bosuil | F. Chouette hulotte | G. Waldkauz | S. Kattuggla

*15 in.

SHORT-EARED OWL

A rather big (38 cm*) long-winged owl seen by daylight in open country is almost certain to be a Short-Eared Owl. Ear-tufts are seldom visible. Eyes golden-yellow. Sexes alike.

Nest on the ground; 4-8 eggs; Apr./May. Incubation (24-28 d.) by hen only but male provides food for the young, which fly when about 4 w. old. Single- (double-) brooded.

Resident breeding locally in Scotland (rarely in Shetlands), N. England and W. Wales, very scarce elsewhere. Winter visitors from the Continent.

Lat. Asio flammeus | D. Velduil | F. Hibou des marais | G. Sumpfohreule | S. Jorduggla

*15 in.

TAWNY OWL

LONG-EARED OWL

A night-time impression

LONG-EARED OWL

Somewhat smaller (33-35 cm*) broad-winged owl with prominent (when perching) ear-tufts and bright yellow eyes. When roosting ear-tufts are laid flat and become invisible. Sexes alike.

Nest in old nest of other birds (exceptionally on the ground); 4-5 eggs; Mch/Apr. Incubation (27-28 d.) by female only but male provides food for the young which fly when about 3 w. old. Single-brooded.

Resident breeding all over British Isles in woody districts though scarce in N. Scotland and rarely in the Shetlands. Only owl breeding commonly in Ireland.

*13-14 in.

Lat. Asio otus | D. Ransuil F. Hibou moyen-duc | G. Waldohreule | S. Hornuggla

SWIFT

Very dark Swallow-like bird (15-17 cm*) with long scythe-like wings and short shallow-forked tail. Has habit of chasing in flocks over towns or villages with a scream-like note. Sexes alike.

Social breeder in holes of roofs of high buildings; 2-3 eggs; May/June. Incubation (18-20 d.) chiefly by female but probably both parents feed young which fly when 5-7 w. old. Single-brooded.

Summer visitor (Apr./Aug.) breeding all over the British Isles (except NW. Scotland Passage-migrants.

*6-7 in.

Lat. Apus apus | D. Gierzwaluw | F. Martinet noir | G. Mauersegler | S. Tornsvala

164

KINGFISHER

Only bird with blue-green upper-parts and warm chestnut under-parts. Long straight black bill reddish at base. Legs red. Sexes alike.

Nest at end of self-bored tunnel in steep banks of streams; 6-7 eggs; Apr./May. Incubation (19-21 d.) and tending of young (fly when 3-4 w. old) by both parents. Double-brooded.

Resident breeding along slow-flowing streams in lowlands of England, Wales, Ireland and S. Scotland. In severe winters moving to the coast.

Lat. Alcedo atthis | D. IJsvogel | F. Martin-pêcheur | G. Eisvogel | S. Kungsfiskare

GREEN WOODPECKER

Largest (30-32 cm*) of British woodpeckers and only green one. Red crown and bright yellow rump. Male has red, black-bordered moustache-like stripe that is all-black in females. Heavy bill grey-black.

Nest in self-bored hole in tree; 5-7 eggs; Apr./June. Incubation (16-18 d.) and tending of young (fly when about 3 w. old) by both parents. Single-brooded.

Resident, breeding in England and Wales and spreading into Scotland.

*12-13 in.

Lat. Picus viridis | D. Groene specht | F. Pic vert | G. Grünspecht | S. Gröngöling

Order PICIFORMES
Family PICIDAE

GREAT SPOTTED WOODPECKER

Rather small (22 cm*) woodpecker with bold pied black back, buffish-white under-parts with crimson under tail-coverts. Male has red nape and juveniles red crown.

Nest in self-bored hole in tree; 4-7 eggs; May/June. Incubation (16-17 d.) mainly by female; young which fly when about 3 w. old are fed by both parents. Single-brooded.

Resident breeding fairly common in England and Wales and S. Scotland. Does not breed in Ireland where only passage-migrant.

*9 in.

Lat. Dendrocopos major | Also: Pied Woodpecker | D. Grote bonte specht | F. Pic épeiche | G. Buntspecht | S. Större hackspett

167

LESSER SPOTTED WOODPECKER

Very small (15 cm*) woodpecker with black and white barred back and wings. No red under tail-coverts. Male has red crown, female whitish, juveniles reddish.

Nest (high) in self-bored hole in tree; 4-6 eggs; May. Incubation (14-15 d.) and tending of young which fly when 3-4 w. old, by both sexes. Single-brooded.

Resident breeding locally in England (very rare in the N.) and Wales. No reliable records from Scotland and Ireland.

*6 in.

Lat. Dendrocopos minor | Also: Barred Woodpecker | D. Kleine bonte specht | F. Pic épeichette | G. Kleinspecht | S. Liten hackspet

WRYNECK

This member of the woodpecker family is small (16cm*) and is brown and grey above and handsomely marked. Underparts are buff, barred with brown; sexes are alike. The name derives from a habit of twisting the head to unusual angles. Nest in hole in tree or bank; 6-10 eggs; May. Summer visitor, in recent years has become rare; mostly seen in south-east England.

Lat. Jynx torquilla torquilla | D. Draaihals | F. Torcol | G. Wendehals | S. Göktyta

*6¾ in.

BLACK WOODPECKER

Larger than Green Woodpecker with all black plumage except for red crown and crest. Thick light coloured bill and yellow eye. Hen has brown tinge with red on nape. Voice is loud and has flute-like double notes as well as single note like Green Woodpecker. Its "drum" is long and loud. Breeding unknown in Great Britain, but vagrants from Continent have often been reported in various parts of England.

This species is not admitted to the British list as the possibility of the birds reported being "escapes" cannot be excluded.

Lat. Dryocopos martius | D. Zwarte Specht | F. Pic noir | G. Schwarzspecht | S. Spillkråka

169

NIGHTJAR

Sometimes called Goatsucker this bird (27 cm*) has perfect camouflage with the ground where it is concealed during the day. It is grey and barred with brown, buff and black. Male has white spots on wings and white tips to outer tail feathers.

Eggs (2) are laid on the ground; May/June; incubation by both sexes (18 days).

Summer visitor, voice recognised by a purring sound like a machine at work.

*10½ in.

Lat. Caprimulgus europaeus | D. Nachtzwaluw | F. Engoulevent | G. Nachtschwalbe | S. Nattskärra

TREE-CREEPER

Small (12½ cm*) brown bird with light under parts; has habit of climbing up (never down) trees hunting for insects, with slender distinctly curved bill. Sexes aiike.

Nest in cracks of trunks, behind loose bark or crevices of buildings; 6-7 eggs; Apr./June. Incubation (18-20 d.) chiefly by female. Both parents feed young which fly when about 2 w. old. Single- (double-) brooded.

Resident breeding all over the British Isles (except Shetlands, Orkneys and O. Hebrides).

*5 in.

Lat. Certhia familiaris | D. Boomkruiper | F. Grimpereau des bois | G. Waldbaumläufer | S. Trädkrypare

NUTHATCH

Sparrow-sized (13 cm*) plump, short-tailed bird with woodpecker-habit of climbing trees. Upper-parts blue-grey, under-parts buff with chestnut flanks. Sexes alike.

Nest in holes of trees and nest boxes of which entrance is narrowed with mud; 6-11 eggs; Apr./May. Only hen incubates (14-15 d.) but both parents feed young which fly when 3-3 ½ w. old. Single-brooded.

Resident, breeding in England and Wales though scarce in N. England. Rare vagrant to Scotland and Ireland.

*5½ in.

Lat. Sitta europaea | D. Boomklever | F. Sittelle | G. Kleiber | S. Nötväcka

WOOD-LARK

Has shorter white-tipped tail, less conspicuous though longer crest and more pronounced eye-stripes (meeting across the nape) than Sky-Lark. Length about 15 cm*. Musical song delivered from fence-posts, tree-tops or in flight and even at night.

Nest on the ground; 3-4 eggs; Mch/May. Incubation (13-14 d.) by female only. Both parents feed young which fly when about 3 w. old. Double-brooded.

Resident, breeding in S. England and Wales. Rare vagrant elsewhere.

*6 in.

Lat. *Lullula arborea* / D. *Boomleeuwerik* / F. *Alouette lulu* / G. *Heidelerche* / S. *Trädlärka*

SKY-LARK

Best field mark is habit of mounting steeply to sing from considerable height. Sky-Lark (17 cm*) differs from Wood-Lark in having longer tail and conspicuous crest. Sexes alike.

Nest on the ground; 3-4 eggs; Apr./June. Incubation`(11-12 d.) by female only but both parents feed young which fly when about 3 w. old. Double-brooded (sometimes three broods).

Breeds commonly all over the British Isles. Most British breeding-birds winter in Europe or Ireland. Migrants from N. Europe winter in England and Ireland. Also passage-migrants from Central Europe.

*7 in.

Lat. Alauda arvensis | D. Veldleeuwerik | F. Alouette des champs | G. Feldlerche | S. Sånglärka

SAND-MARTIN

Small (10-12½ cm*) swallow with slightly forked tail. Upper-parts brown, under-parts white with brown band across the breast. Sexes alike.

Social breeder in self-bored holes in sand-pits and steep banks of rivers; 4-5 eggs; May/July. Incubation (13-14 d.) and tending of young by both sexes. Young fly when about 3 w. old. Double-brooded.

Summer visitor (Mch/Sept.) breeding all over the British Isles, but scarce in N. Scotland.
Colour picture page 177

*4-5 in.

Lat. Riparia riparia | N. Am. Bank Swallow | D. Oever-zwaluw | F. Hirondelle de rivage | G. Uferschwalbe | S. Backsvala

SWALLOW

Deeply forked tail, blue-black upper-parts and chestnut throat and fore-head are characteristic. No white rump. Juveniles have less deeply forked tail. Sexes alike (18 cm*).

Nest open, saucer-shaped, built (by both sexes) of mud; 4-5 eggs; May/Aug. Incubation (14-15 d.) by female only. Both parents feed young which fly when about 3 w. old. Double-brooded (sometimes three broods).

Summer visitor (Apr./Oct.) breeding all over the British Isles, though scarce in NW. Scotland and isles.

*7½ in.

Lat. Hirundo rustica | N. Am. Barn Swallow | D. Boerenzwaluw | F. Hirondelle de cheminée | G. Rauchschwalbe | S. Ladusvala

HOUSE-MARTIN

Much like Swallow but conspicuous white rump, less deeply forked tail and lack of chestnut at throat exclude confusion. Length about 12½ cm* tail included.

Social breeder under eaves in cup-shaped nests built (by both sexes) of mud; 4-5 eggs; May/Aug. Incubation (14-15 d.) and tending of young (fly when about 3 w. old) by both sexes. Two (three) broods.

Summer visitor (Apr./Oct.) breeding all over the British Isles (locally in Ireland, scarce in I. Hebrides and Orkneys, seldom in the Shetlands; rare vagrant to O. Hebrides).

Lat. Delichon urbica | D. Huiszwaluw | F. Hirondelle de fenêtre | G. Mehlschwalbe | S. Hussvala

*5 in.

Left: Sand-Martin; Right: House-Martin

GOLDEN ORIOLE

About Thrush-size. Male bright yellow with black wings and tail. Female (and immature birds) yellowish-green, wings and tail darker. Length 22-25 cm*.

Nest in fork of small branch; 3-4 eggs; May/June. Incubation (14-15 d.) and tending of young (fly when about 2 w. old) by both parents. Single-brooded.

Scarce and irregular passage-migrant in April and May, more regularly in SW. and SE. England. Occasionally, breeding in southern counties.

*9-10 in.

Lat. Oriolus oriolus | D. Wielewaal | F. Loriot | G. Pirol | S. Sommargylling

ROOK

ROOK (right) and JACKDAW (see page 186)

Much like Carrion Crow but slenderer bill, black plumage with purplish gloss, wings longer, baggy appearance of thigh-feathers. Adults have greyish-white face. Sexes alike (45 cm*).

Social breeder in large trees; 3-5 eggs; Mch/Apr. Female alone incubates (16-18 d.) but both parents feed young which fly when about 4 w. old. Single-brooded.

Resident breeding all over Britain (including Shetlands, since 1952). Many migrants arrive at E. coast in autumn to winter in England or Scotland.

*18 in

Lat. Corvus frugilegus | D. Roek | F. Corbeau freux | G. Saatkrähe | S. Råka

JAY

Least crow-like of Corvidae, but blue wing-patch, white rump and black tail, in combination with size (33 cm*) and harsh voice are distinctive. Rather conspicuous crest. Sexes alike.

Nest in small trees or bushes; 5-6 eggs; May/June. Incubation (16-17 d.) mainly by female. Both parents feed young which fly when about 3 w. old. Single-brooded.

Resident, breeding commonly in England and Wales, very local in Scotland. In Ireland a somewhat darker plumage: G.g. hibernicus.

*13 in.

Lat. Garrulus glandarius | D. Vlaamse gaai | F. Geai des chênes | G. Eichelhäher | S. Nötskrika

JAY

View from the back

MAGPIE

A winter impression

MAGPIE

Black and white plumage combined with size (45 cm* including long tail) are distinctive. Usually seen in pairs or small parties. Sexes alike.

Domed nest in tall trees or bushes; 5-8 eggs; Apr./May. Incubation (17-18 d.) by female only but both parents feed young which fly when 3-4 w. old. Single-brooded.

Resident breeding commonly, though often locally, all over the British Isles. Very scarce in N. Scotland.

*18 in.

Lat. Pica pica | D. Ekster | F. Pie bavarde | G. Elster | S. Skata

HOODED CROW

Typical crow whose grey mantle and under-parts exclude confusion with other species. Length 45-47 cm*. Sexes alike.

Nest in trees or bushes; 4-6 eggs; Mch/Apr. Incubation (19-20 d.) by female only but male assists in feeding of young which fly when 4-5 w. old. Single-brooded.

Resident breeding in N. Scotland, Ireland and the Isle of Man. In England and Wales (scarce) winter visitor (Oct./Apr.). Mixed pairs of Hooded Crow and Carrion-Crow occur where breeding ranges of both overlap.

*18-19 in.

Lat. Corvus cornix | D. Bonte kraai | F. Corneille mantelée | G. Nebelkrähe | S. Grå kråka

Order PASSERIFORMES Family CORVIDAE

RAVEN

Biggest (63 cm*) of crow-tribe all-black with heavy bill and wedge-shaped tail. Sexes alike.

Big nest built by both sexes; 4-6 eggs; Febr./ Mch. Female broods (20-21 d.) and is fed by male. Both parents feed young which fly when 5-6 w. old. Single-brooded.

Resident breeding in fair numbers along coasts of England (not E. coast between Moray and Kent), Wales, Scotland and Ireland and also inland.

Lat. Corvus corax | D. Raaf | F. Grand corbeau | G. Kolkrabe | S. Korp

*25 in.

CARRION-CROW

All-black but smaller (45-47 cm*) than Raven and differing from Hooded Crow in having shorter, broader wings, shorter tail, greenish gloss on plumage. See also Rook. Sexes alike.

Nest in tall trees, bushes or on cliff-ledges; 4-5 eggs; Apr./June. Only female incubates (18-20 d.) but young are fed by both parents. They fly when 4-5 w. old. Single-brooded.

Resident, breeding in England, Wales and S. and E. Scotland.

*18-19 in.

Lat. Corvus corone | D. Zwarte kraai | F. Corneille noire | G. Rabenkrähe | S. Svart kråka

JACKDAW (illustration p. 179)

Small (33 cm*) but typical crow whose grey nape excludes confusion with other species. Black bill and legs. Sexes alike.

Tends to social nesting in holes of trees, walls and rocks; 4-6 eggs; Apr./May. Only hen incubates (17-18 d.) but both parents feed young which fly when 4-5 w. old. Single-brooded.

Resident breeding all over Britain except O. Hebrides and Shetland, though scarce in NW. Scotland. There seems to be some migration and many birds from the Continent winter here.

*13 in.

Lat. Corvus monedula | D. Kauwtje | F. Choucas des tours | G. Dohle | S. Kaja

CHOUGH

Slightly larger than jackdaw (40 cm*) but has glossy black plumage, long curved scarlet bill and scarlet legs.

Nest of sticks in a crevasse on a cliff; 3-6 eggs; April/May.

Resident, now very rare, only to be found in west Ireland, Wales and Scotland, and south-west England.

*16 in.

Lat. Pyrrhocorax pyrrhocorax / *D. Alpenkraai* / *F. Crave à bec rouge* /*G. Alpenkrähe* / *S. Alpkråka*

HOOPOE

This striking and unusual bird will never be mistaken once seen, for it is unlike any other bird. The prominent crest (which can be fanned out or laid back on the head), gives it an exotic appearance. The head, neck and breast are all of a pinkish hue, the rump and belly white, the back wings and bill are barred black and white. The bill is long, pointed and curved.

Its cry—"hoo-hoo-hoo"—also distinguishes it.

Spring visitor in small numbers to S. and E. England, where it has occasionally bred.

Latin. Upupa epops | D. Hop | F. Huppe | G. Wiedehopf | S. Härfågel

NOTES

Bird watching is a matter of using our opportunities where-ever we happen to be. The late Field Marshal Lord Alan-brooke, who was a great bird lover, tells in his story of the war how he would slip away from a top level conference to study the birds nearby. He found this a great relaxation. By using such like opportunities we will find that there are few places that offer no chances for bird watching, even in the heart of towns and cities.

Wood Pigeons are to be found all over Britain, both in the countryside and in towns. As a matter of fact, if we cannot spend much time on watching birds it is a good thing to choose for our studies a species that is common; if we choose a rare bird, we will waste much time in travelling to and from its breeding site.

Prof. Joseph J. Hickey in *A Guide to Bird Watching* tells how a

Dr. G. K. Noble wrote a very interesting article on the courtship and breeding behaviour of a pair of woodpeckers. These birds nested in a tree of Dr. Noble's bathroom and he made all his observations while having a morning shave! The Cuckoo is another species whose habits have been carefully studied; a lot of secrets of the Cuckoo remain to be revealed. The least we can do is to keep note of the date on which we hear our first Cuckoo in spring.

Owls are more difficult to study because of their nocturnal habits. However both Little Owl and Short-eared Owl can often be seen in daytime and most species start hunting for mice in twilight. Time and again the loud and excited calls of small birds may guide us to a Tawny Owl or Little Owl that is being mobbed.

The Nightjar is another species with mainly nocturnal habits. In heath country we have a fair chance to hear its remarkable vibrant, reeling song, that is most usually heard around dusk and dawn. It is often kept up for minutes on end (it might be a good idea to time the length of each "purr" with a stopwatch). One of the features of the call is that it alternates sharply between two distinct pitches.

The severe winter of 1963 has caused an alarming decrease of the numbers of Kingfishers. Whereas other species seem to have recovered fairly well, the Kingfishers have been slow in re-establishing.

The Hoopoe is but a straggler to Britain. In the first half of this century the species seemed to be rapidly disappearing from countries in Western Europe, where it had been more or less abundant. Since the war an increase has been noted, that may explain the growing number of observations in the British Isles.

All species of the Woodpecker tribe are easily recognised. Most of them are fairly common. They have the habit of drumming on a dead branch or even on a nest box in spring. The Green Woodpecker drums rather less, but this bird has a loud neighing call. This species is very fond of ants and their puppae and can often be seen on lawns, gorging on them.

The Black Woodpecker has been observed repeatedly in Britain. Its exclusion from the British List is only due to the fact that the possibility of the birds seen being "escapes" could not be excluded.

The Crow family includes a number of highly individualistic members, the common Rook in his colony high in a tree offers a most interesting study of bird behaviour, for there is always something fresh to note. Rooks appear to be the most intelligent of birds. They will no longer nest in a tree which is threatened with rot or disease. The Jackdaw is a most delightful bird, that can be tamed easily as a pet and offers opportunities for any amount of experiments. Most of the crows seem to pair for life, in sharp contrast to many small songbirds, which often change partners between the first brood and the next.

5

TITS, THRUSHES AND WARBLERS

Long-tailed Tits in flight

5

PASSERIFORMES

FAMILIES REPRESENTED
IN PART 5

Paridae	Tits
Turdinae	Thrushes
Troglodytidae	Wrens
Sylviinae	Warblers
Cinclidae	Dippers

TITS, THRUSHES AND WARBLERS

The families represented in part 5 are mainly the Paridae (Tits), the Turdinae (Thrushes) and the Sylviinae (Warblers). The handsome Tit family is resident and the family likeness runs through all the members so that recognition is never difficult.

The Thrush family covers a diverse range from the Thrush, Blackbird and Robin which are resident, to the Redwing and Fieldfare, (winter visitors), and the Wheatear, Chats, Redstarts and Nightingale which are summer visitors. The Black Redstart is the most rare being mainly a Continental bird which visits the south-eastern part of the country, and in fact it has been known to colonise bombed sites in the centre of London.

The Sylviinae do not differ to the same extent — indeed there is a striking similarity in shape, size and general characteristics. It is because of this strong family ressemblance that identification is difficult and in some cases the differences are very subtle. It is recommended that the bird watcher first becomes familiar with the more common members of the family and recognition of the rarer ones will follow.

WILLOW TIT

Very similar to Marsh Tit, with dull instead of glossy black cap. Call is nasal, harshly slurred "zi-zurr-zurr-zurr". Sexes alike.

Nest in self-bored hole in rotten wood; 8-9 eggs; Apr./May. Only hen incubates (13-14 d.); both parents feed young which fly when 17-19 d. old. Single-brooded.

Resident, breeding locally in England, Wales and Scotland. Unknown in Ireland.

Lat. Parus atricapillus | N. Am. Chickadee | D. Matkopmees | F. Mésange boréale | G. Weidenmeise | S. Talltita

BEARDED TIT

This rare reedling (15½ cm*) is easily recognised by those who are fortunate enough to see it, on account of its wedge-shaped tail and light red and grey plumage. Male has a blue-grey head and a prominent black moustache from whence it gets its name. The wings are striped, and the female is duller in tone, and has no moustache.

Nest above the water; eggs 5-7; April/July.

Resident, only in East Anglia.

*6¼ in.

Latin. Panurus biarmicus biarmicus | D. Baardmannetje | F. Mésange à moustache | G. Bartmeise | S. Skäggmes

Order PASSERIFORMES
Family PARIDAE

COAL TIT

Even smaller (9 cm*) than Blue Tit, head-pattern as Great Tit, but conspicuous white patch on the nape, under-parts buff; double white wing-bar, short tail. Young birds have yellow under-parts but also yellow cheeks. Sexes alike.

Nest in hole of tree (close to the ground) or bank; 7-11 eggs; Apr./ May. Incubation (14-16 d.) by hen only; both parents feed young which fly when 16-17 d. old. Single-brooded.

Resident, breeding all over the British Isles though unknown in the Shetlands, Orkneys and O. Hebrides. Irish Coal Tits have yellowish cheeks and patch on the nape (P.a. hibernicus).

*4¼ in.

Lat. Parus ater | D. Zwarte mees | F. Mésange noire | G. Tannenmeise |S. Svartmes

CRESTED TIT

Small (10 cm*) tit with distinctive crest which excludes confusion with any other member of tit-tribe. Sexes alike.

Nest in self-bored holes in decayed pine-wood; 5-6 eggs; Apr./May. Only female incubates (13-15 d.), both parents feed young which fly when 17-18 d. old. Single-brooded.

Resident breeding in the Scottish Highlands only, especially in the Spey Valley.

*4½ in.

Lat. Parus cristatus / D. Kuifmees / F. Mésange huppée / G. Haubenmeise / S. Tofsmes

MARSH TIT

Small (10 cm*) titmouse with glossy black crown. No white patch on the nape, no wing-bar, cheeks pale but not white. Very much like Willow Tit, difference in notes being practically only safe distinction. "Pitchuu" is the note of Marsh Tit. Sexes alike.

Nest in holes of trees (sometimes walls or nest-boxes); 7-8 eggs; Apr./May. Incubation (13-14 d.) by female only; both parents feed young which fly when 16-18 d. old. Single- (double-) brooded.

Resident, breeding in England and Wales (local in Cornwall, Cumberland and NW. Wales). In Scotland only in Berwick; unknown in Ireland.

*4½ in.

Lat. Parus palustris | D. Glanskopmees | F. Mésange nonnette | G. Sumpfmeise | S. Kärrmes

LONG-TAILED TIT

Very small (13 cm* including 7½ cm**-tail) like ball of wool with knitting-needles (tail) put into it. Head white with black eye-stripe, under-parts pinkish-white, back and wings blackish with pink. Sexes alike.

Domed nest of moss, lichen, cobwebs and hair built by both sexes; 8-12 eggs; Apr./May. Incubation (14-16 d.) by female; both parents feed young which fly when 15-16 d. old. Single-brooded.

Resident breeding all over the British Isles, but almost unknown in the O. Hebrides, Orkneys and Shetlands.

*5½ in.   **3 in.

Lat. Aegithalos caudatus | D. Staartmees | F. Mésange à longue queue | G. Schwanzmeise | S. Stjärtmes

BLUE TIT

Small (10 cm*) short-tailed tit with bright blue crown, white face, green mantle and yellow under-parts. Sexes alike.

Nest in holes of trees, walls and nest-boxes; 7-14 eggs; Apr./May. Only female incubates (13-14 d.) but both sexes feed young which fly when 18-20 d. old. Single-brooded.

Resident breeding commonly in Britain though scarce in NW. Scotland.

*4½ in.

Lat. Parus caeruleus | D. Pimpelmees | F. Mésange bleue | G. Blaumeise | S Blåmes

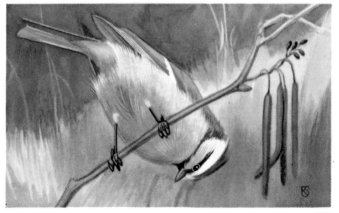

GREAT TIT

About Sparrow-size (13 cm*). Bright yellow under-parts, green mantle, black and white head, broad black bib (biggest in male). Sexes almost alike.

Nest in hole of tree, wall or nest-box; 5-11 eggs; Apr./May. Only female incubates (13-14 d.) but both parents feed young which fly when 18-21 d. old. Single-brooded.

Resident, breeding all over British Isles though rather scarce in N. and W. Scotland.

*5½ in.

Lat. Parus major | D. Koolmees | F. Mésange charbonnière | G. Kohlmeise | S. Talgoxe

GREAT TIT

Side view

Order PASSERIFORMES   *Family TURDINAE*

FIELDFARE

Somewhat like Thrush but blue-grey head, nape and rump, contrasting with chestnut back and wings and blackish tail are distinctive. In flight white under-wings and "arm-pits" like Mistle-Thrush. Length about 25 cm*. Sexes alike.

Passage-migrant and winter visitor (Oct./Apr.) all over the British Isles. Highly gregarious, often associated with Redwings, feeding nearly always in the open though seldom far from cover.

Lat. Turdus pilaris | D. Kramsvogel | F. Grive litorne | G. Wacholderdrossel | S. Björktrast

WREN

Order PASSERIFORMES.
Family
TROGLODYTIDAE

WREN

Very small (9½ cm*), russet-brown bird with short, usually cocked-up tail. Male sings nearly all year round. Sexes alike.

Domed nest of moss, grass and leaves is lined with feathers; 5-7 eggs; Apr. / May. Incubation (14-15 d.) by female only, but both parents feed young which fly when 16-18 d. old. Double-brooded. One male may have two or even three wives at the same time.

Resident, breeding all over the British Isles. In the Shetlands breeds T.t. zetlandicus; in the O. Hebrides T.t. hebridensis in St Kilda T.t. hirtensis.

*3¾ in.

Lat. Troglodytes troglodytes | D. Winterkoninkje | F. Troglodyte | G. Zaunkönig | S. Gärdsmyg

MISTLE-THRUSH

Slightly bigger (25-27cm*) but very much like Song Thrush. Long tail with whitish tips to outer feathers. White under-wings and "arm-pits". Dark spots on breast bigger than in Thrush. No eye-stripe. Sexes alike.

Nest usually in fork of tree; 4 eggs; March/May. Incubation (13-14 d.) by hen only; both parents feed young which fly when about 2 w. old. Double-brooded.

Resident, breeding all over the British Isles though scarce in NW. Scotland and rare in the Orkneys. Northern birds tend to move S. in autumn.

*10-11 in.

Lat. Turdus viscivorus / D. Grote lijster / F. Grive draine / G. Misteldrossel / S. Dubbeltrast

Order PASSERIFORMES
Subfamily TURDINAE

SONG-THRUSH

Smaller (22 cm*) than Mistle-Thrush with shorter tail, breast with smaller spots, upper-parts warmer brown. Under-wing and "arm-pits" golden-buff. Sexes alike.

Nest in hedgerows, bushes and trees; 4-5 eggs; Apr./June. Only female incubates (13-14 d.); both parents feed young which fly when about 2 w. old. Double-brooded.

Resident, breeding all over the British Isles. Part of the British Thrushes move S. in autumn when winter-visitors from the Continent (belonging to the race T.p. philomelos) arrive on E. coast.

*9 in.

Lat. Turdus philomelos | Also: Throstle | D. Zanglijster | F. Grive musicienne | G. Singdrossel | S. Taltrast

REDWING

Small (21 cm*) typical thrush, that can easily be told from other thrushes by chestnut-red flanks and under-wing and conspicuous light eye-stripe. Sexes alike. Highly gregarious (often with Field-fares).

Passage-migrant and winter visitor (Sept./Apr.) which has exceptionally bred in N. Scotland and Fair Isle.

*8¼ in.

Lat. Turdus iliacus / D. Koperwiek / F. Grive mauvis / G. Rotdrossel / S. Rödvingetrast

RED WING

Front view

BLACKBIRD
Side view of male

FIELDFARE

BLACKBIRD

All-black plumage combined with yellow bill of cock are distinctive. Females and juveniles have uppper-parts dark-brown and under-parts mottled. Length about 25 cm*. One of our commonest song-birds.

Nest in bushes, hedges, and even on window-sills; 4-5 eggs; Apr./June. Incubation (12-14 d.) chiefly by hen; both parents feed young which fly when about 2 w. old. Two/three broods.

Resident all over the British Isles. Winter visitors from the Continent.

*10 in.

Lat. Turdus merula | D. Merel | F. Merle noir | G. Amsel | S. Koltrast

WHEATEAR

Sparrow-sized (14 cm*) bird with conspicuous white rump. Nearly always seen on the ground in open country. Male with bold black cheeks.

Nest in hole in the ground (rabbit-burrows), in walls or drainpipes; 5-6 eggs; Apr./May Incubation (14 d.) chiefly by female; both sexes feed young which fly when about 2 w. old. Single-brooded.

Summer visitor (Mch/ Oct.) breeding all over the British Isles.

*5¾ in.

*Lat. Oenanthe oenanthe /
D. Tapuit / F. Tracquet
motteux / G. Steinschmät-
zer / S. Stenskvätta*

WHEATEAR

The white rump is conspicuous in flight
(See picture opposite)

REDSTART

Redstarts are small birds with chestnut-red tails which constantly move. Male common Redstart (14 cm*) has black face and throat and white fore-head. Females and juveniles are very difficult to tell from those of Black Redstarts.

Nest in hole of tree or wall or nest box; 5-6 eggs; May/July. Incubation chiefly by female (12-14 d.); both parents feed young which fly when about 2 w. old. Often double-brooded.

Summer visitor (Apr./Oct.) breeding in fluctating numbers in most parts of England, Wales and Scottish mainland, but very rarely in Ireland and passage- migrant or vagrant elsewhere.

*5½ in.

Lat. Phoenicurus phoenicurus / D. Gekraagde roodstaart / F. Rougequeue à front blanc / G. Gartenrotschwanz / S. Rödstjärt

REDSTART

Side view

BLACK REDSTART

Has typical Redstart-tail but lacks orange under-parts and white fore-head of common Redstart, being very dark bird (14 cm*) having breast black as well as throat and face and only white patch on the wings. Female and juveniles are very much like those of common Redstarts though somewhat darker.

Nest in hole or on ledge of building or rock; 4-6 eggs; Apr./July. Only female incubates (12-14 d.); both parents feed young which fly when about 2½ w. old. Two (three) broods.

Summer visitor (Mch/Nov.). Has colonized bombed sites in Inner London and has bred in Middlesex and Sussex. Migrants pass along E. coast of England and through Ireland. Small numbers winter in S. and SW. England, W. Wales and S. Ireland.

*5½ in.

Lat. Phoenicurus ochruros | D. Zwarte roodstaart | F. Rougequeue noir | G. Hausrotschwanz | S. Svart rödstjärt

Order PASSERIFORMES
Subfamily TURDINAE

WHINCHAT

Conspicuous white eye-stripe. Black cheeks with white mark below are distinctive for red-breasted, male Whinchat (12½ cm*) Females and juveniles resemble Stone-chats but have also distinct though duller eye-stripes.

Nest on the ground in high grass; 5-6 eggs; May/July. Only hen incubates (13-14 d.); both sexes feed young which fly when about 2 w. old. Single- (double-) brood-ed.

Summer visitor Apr./Oct. to all parts of British Isles, though not breeding in W. Cornwall and Shetlands and scarce in the Orkneys, O. Hebrides and S. half of Ireland.

*5 in.

Lat. Saxicola rubetra | D. Paapje | F. Tracquet tarier | G. Braunkehlchen | S. Buskskvätta

223

STONECHAT

Black-headed, red-breasted bird with white patch on the sides of the neck. No eye-stripe. No white in tail. Female and young resemble Whinchat but lack white eye-stripe. Likes to perch on tops of bushes, fence-posts and wires. Length about 12½ cm*.

Nest on or near the ground; 5-6 eggs; Mch/July. Incubation (14-15 d.) by female only; both sexes feed young which fly when about two w. old. Double-brooded.

Resident, breeding all over the British Isles, commonest in coastal regions, rarely breeding in the Orkneys and only occasional visitor to the Shetlands. Birds breeding in the N. move S. in autumn.

*5 in.

Lat. Saxicola torquata
D. Roodborsttapuit
F. Tracquet pâtre.
G. Schwarzkehlchen
S. Svarthakad buskskvätta

ROBIN

This well-known little bird (14 cm*) with its bright red breast, throat and fore-head is one of our commonest garden-birds. Juveniles have speckled breast. Sexes alike.

Nest in hole in bank, tree or wall or even old tins; 4-6 eggs; Mch/June. Only female incubates (13-14 d.); both parents feed young which fly when about 2 w. old. Two (three) broods.

Resident, breeding commonly all over the British Isles (except Shetlands) though scarce in N. Scotland and the Orkneys. British birds (E.r. melophilus cannot be separated in the field from the Continental (E.r. rubecula) which winters here.

*5½ in.

Lat. Erithacus rubecula | D. Roodborstje | F. Rougegorge | G. Rotkehlchen | S. Rödhake

NIGHTINGALE

Rufous-brown bird (16½ cm*) with reddish tail recognized by its well-known song. Has typical thrush-silhouette. Sexes alike.

Nest on or close to the ground among nettles and other tall weeds; 4-5 eggs; May/June. Incubation (13-14 d.) by hen only; both parents feed young which fly when about 2 w. old. Single-brooded.

Summer visitor, breeding commonly in S. and E. England, very locally in SE. Wales.

*6½ in.

Lat. Luscinia megarhynchos / D. Nachtegaal / F. Rossignol / G. Nachtigall / S. Sydlig näktergal

ICTERINE WARBLER

Rather big (14 cm*) among warblers, with pale-yellow under-parts, olive-brown upper-parts, bluish grey legs and long pointed wings. Inside of mouth orange-red. Sexes alike.

Though the Icterine Warbler is a common breeding-bird in W. Europe, it is only a rare vagrant to Britain in spring and (more often) autumn on E. coast. (Has bred in Wiltshire).

*5½ in.

Lat. Hippolais icterina / D. Spotvogel / F. Hypolaïs ictérine / G. Gartenspötter S. Bastardnäktergal

Order PASSERIFORMES
Subfamily SYLVIINAE

BLACKCAP

Glossy black cap of male and reddish-brown of female and juveniles are distinctive. Only other small birds with black caps are Marsh- and Willow-tits, which also have black chins and are smaller.

Nest in bushes or hedgerows; 4-5 eggs; May/June. Incubation (10-11 d.) and tending of young by both sexes. Young fly when 10-13 d. old. Single- (double-) brooded.

Mainly summer visitor (Apr./Oct.). Breeds in England, Wales and S. counties of Scotland (N. to the Spey Valley).

Lat. Sylvia atricapilla | D. Zwartkopje | F. Fauvette à tête noire |G. Mönchsgrasmücke | S. Svarthätta

228

SEDGE-WARBLER

Typical warbler (12½ cm*) with broad creamy eye-stripe and streaked crown and mantle. Tawny rump without streaks. Under-parts creamy-white. Sexes alike.

Nest mostly near water in tall weeds or bushes; 5-6 eggs; May/June. Incubation (13-14 d.) chiefly by female; both parents feed young which fly when about 2 w. old. Single- (double-) brooded.

Summer visitor (Apr./Sept.) breeding fairly commonly in England, Wales and Ireland; less common in Scotland.

*5 in.

Lat. Acrocephalus schoenobaenus | D. Rietzanger | F. Phragmite des joncs | G. Schilfrohrsänger | S. Sävsångare

REED-WARBLER

Slender unobtrusive bird (12½ cm*) with near-white throat. No black markings on brown upper-parts, no eye-stripe, no streaks on light buff under-parts. Best field-mark is song. Sexes alike.

Nest is deep cup woven by female between reeds; 4-5 eggs; June/July. Incubation (11 d.) and tending of young by both parents. Young fly when 11-12 d. old. Single- (double-) brooded.

Summer visitor (Apr./Sept.) breeding fairly common in S. and mid-England, very locally in S. and SE. Wales, only rare vagrant to Scotland and Ireland.

*5 in.

Lat. Acrocephalus scirpaceus | D. Kleine karekiet | F. Rousserolle effarvatte | G. Teichrohrsänger | S. Rörsangare

WHITETHROAT

No other warbler has rufous wings. Male Whitethroat has grey head and conspicuous white throat. No dark ear-coverts. Rather poor song is also very characteristic.

Nest in low bushes and rank vegetation; 4-5 eggs; May/July. Both sexes incubate (11-13 d.) and feed young which fly when 10-12 d. old. Double-brooded.

Summer visitor (Apr./Oct.) breeding all over the British Isles, though local in N. Scotland and rare in O. Hebrides, being a passage-migrant only in the Orkneys and Shetlands.

Lat. Sylvia communis / D. Grasmus / F. Fauvette grisette / G. Dorngrasmücke / S. Törnsångare

LESSER WHITETHROAT

Sligthly smaller (13 cm*) than Whitethroat with dark patch behind the eye. No rufous wings but otherwise much like common Whitethroat though song is quite different.

Nest in hedges or bushes; 4-6 eggs; May/June. Incubation chiefly by female (10-11 d.); both parents feed young which fly when about 11 d. old. Single-brooded.

Summer visitor (Apr./Oct.) breeding fairly common in S. England, Midlands and E. Wales (not Cornwall). Has bred in several counties in Scotland. Rare vagrant to Ireland.

*5¼ in.

Lat. Sylvia curruca | D. Braamsluiper | F. Fauvette babillarde | G. Zaungrasmücke | S. Ärtsångare

Order PASSERIFORMES   *Subfamily SYLVIINAE*

GRASSHOPPER WARBLER

Small and inconspicuous, this green-brown warbler is very secretive and needs much patient observation. It is distinctive from the other warblers on account of its strongly mottled plumage. Once you have come to know its grasshopper-like song, you will discover that it is not rare at all in the south.

Nest of grass and moss in undergrowth or bush; eggs 4-6; May/April.

Summer visitor; favours downland, heaths and marshes.

Latin. Locustella naevia | D. Sprinkhaanrietzanger | F. Locustelle tachetée | G. Heuschreckenrohsanger | S. Gräshoppsångare

GARDEN-WARBLER

Rather negative features (no black cap, no light throat, no eyestripe). Has sweet musical song, summer visitor. Very secretive bird. Sexes alike.

Nest in shrubs or trees or even tall weeds; 4-5 eggs; May/June. Incubation chiefly by female (12-13 d.); both parents feed young which fly when only 9-10 d. old. Single-brooded.

Summer visitor (Apr./Oct.) breeding in England, Wales, S. Scotland and very local in Ireland.

Lat. Sylvia borin | D. Tuinfluiter | F. Fauvette des jardins | G. Gartengrasmücke | S. Trädgårdsångare

DIPPER

Small (17 cm*) bird of rocky streams and burns; in shape like a large wren; its dark plumage, white breast and throat make it most outstanding. Head dark brown and chestnut band across the belly. Has a habit of bobbing and dipping by the water. Seen both on and under the water.

Domed nest of moss and leaves in a cliff in the rock or a hole in the bank; 4/6 eggs; April/June.

Resident and breeding in hill districts of the West and North. Continental birds, sometimes winter in South and East England.

*7 in.

Lat. Cinclus cinclus / *D. Waterspreeuw* / *F. Cincle plongeur* / *G. Wasseramsel* / *S. Strömstare*

NOTES

The most familiar birds are in the Order *Passeriformes* because many of them are to be seen at any hour of the day in the garden or near our homes and the first start in bird study should be made here. They include the Tits, Blackbird, Song Thrush, Robin, Whitethroat, Sparrow and the Finches. There is an abundance of interest to be found in our immediate surroundings and we should familiarise ourselves with the birds there and study their habits and their notes.

The birds in this order are our most notable songsters and often recognition is easiest made through their voices. We need to separate the note of the Blackbird from that of the Song Thrush; to pick out the sweet voice of the Robin and know the repertoire of the Starling, for this bird is certainly the one with the widest range of notes.

If we go into the woods it is important to know the screech of the Jay, the laughing cry of the Green Woodpecker and the Magpie's chatter. Wider afield in the Spring and Summer we can rejoice in the song of the Skylark and be amused by the Yellowhammer's song "Little bit of bread and no cheese".

We usually know of the arrival of the summer visitors by their song. The Cuckoo and the Chiff-Chaff and Willow Wren are three we may hear before we see them. The same can mostly be said of the Warblers. These are small birds which enrich our lives by their voices. Much of the fascination of bird study lies in the ability to put a name to a voice and in spring and summer especially the recognition of bird notes is most necessary.

It is also essential to bear in mind that some of our summer visitors just pass through some localities on the way to their breeding grounds. A case in point is the Wheatear which frequents and breeds on the moors of the North and in consequence is only seen in some areas of the South on its way in the Spring or on its return journey in the Autumn. A special watch can be kept for such birds at these particular seasons.

Some years our winter visitors, perhaps because of the weather, frequent a locality where they are rarely seen. Flocks of Fieldfares for instance may only visit a place once every few years and their striking appearance will cause most people to notice them.

It is this element of surprise, never knowing what may have the good fortune to see that makes bird spotting such an absorbing study. It is a matter of using time, eyes and ears to discover one of the most satisfying and rewarding of interests.

Dippers are most numerous in parts of the Highlands, where they start nesting very early and as soon as the young have fledged the families split up, each individual fishing its own beat of a burn. These birds can often be found near waterfalls and it is fascinating to see them going underwater to chase their food, a most unusual habit in songbirds.

Every time we observe the wren we are surprised that so tiny a bird can produce so shattering a sound. When studying its habits we may find, that one cock may have bonds with up to four or five hens and wonder that it can still find time for its frequent loud bursts of song.

It may seem an omission in this book that no effort is made to give verbal description of the songs or calls of the birds. As there was only a very limited space available for the text, these descriptions were left out intentionally. Though some authors of bird books have made admirable achievements when trying to describe bird song verbally, I still feel (apart from such cases as the Cuckoo) that more often than not these descriptions are intelligible only to those who are already well versed with the characteristics of the song. The best way to learn the song of a bird is to get so near to it that it is possible to recognise the bird by its plumage. Then we should try to memorise characteristic parts of its song that will enable us to recognise it when we hear it again, without even seeing the bird.

However, excellent gramophone records are now available which offer us a chance of studying bird song even in winter-time when the performer itself is actually catching caterpillars in an equatorial forest. These gramophone records can be listened to time and again, until we are certain that we know the song well enough to be able to isolate them from the morning chorus of a fine spring day (See page 292).

Wren's nest

6

WAGTAILS, BUNTINGS AND FINCHES

Goldfinch on Thistledown

6

PASSERIFORMES (CONTINUED)

FAMILIES REPRESENTED
IN PART 6

Sylviinae	Warblers
Regulidae	Kinglets
Muscicapinae	Flycatchers
Prunellidae	Accentors
Motacillidae	Wagtails
Laniidae	Shrikes
Sturnidae	Starling
Fringillidae	Finches
Bombycillidae	Waxwings
Emberizidae	Buntings
Ploceidae	Sparrows

WAGTAILS, BUNTINGS AND FINCHES

In the following pages we continue with the last of the Warblers, followed by the Goldcrest and Firecrest which are the tiniest birds in Britain. They often associate with the Tits which they resemble in some respects although the bold colours of their crests assure identification.

Flycatchers and Hedge Sparrows are unobtrusive birds and consequently unfamiliar, although the Hedge Sparrow is very common. Pipits show a greater likeness to the Skylark than to the closely related Wagtails which can be confusing until one becomes familiar with both.

Few birds have such a striking family appearance as the Wagtails (Motacillidae). The Shrike is known to schoolboys as the "butcher bird".

The common Starling and the Chaffinch are known to everyone for the latter is one of the most numerous birds. The Finches are one of the largest families and show some likeness to the Buntings. The Finches offer less problems in recognition; of the Buntings, the three commonest are dealt with as well as some rarer species. Finally there are the House Sparrow and the Tree Sparrow. The House Sparrow is the best known bird both in town and country, though it is not the most numerous as townspeople often believe.

Bird spotting, absorbing hobby though it may be, is never an end in itself. It should be the means of starting a study of bird behaviour and of gaining bird knowledge. There is no more satisfying or delightful study than that of ornithology, particularly if we go deeper into the subject, find out by our own observation the wonderful ways of birds, and experience for ourselves all the charm and all the beauty in this realm of nature.

These books follow mainly the Wetmore order of classification. Technical reasons of printing production, however, have made some rearrangement necessary (See also Appendix on page 284).

WAXWING

The crest, yellow tip on tail and the red white and yellow markings on the wings, make this an easily recognised bird. It has a black patch on the throat and a grey rump, while the main plumage is a pinkish brown. Often seen in small flocks and feeds on the berries of a great variety of trees and shrubs.

Irregular winter visitor to many parts of Britain; occasionally large numbers come over from the Continent.

Latin. Bombycilla garrulus / D. Pestvogel / F. Jaseur de Bohème / G. Seidenschwanz / S. Sidensvans

DARTFORD WARBLER

This small warbler (12½ cm*) is dark-brown above and a reddish hue underneath. In winter it has reddish marks on the throat. Female is lighter in tone and both have a long tail. Has a distinctive triple call note.

Nest of dry grass, lined with hair or wool in gorse bushes or heather; eggs 3-4(5); April/July. Incubation (12d.) chiefly by female; both parents feed young which fly when about 2 w. old. Two (three) broods.

It is the only resident warbler and found only in some southern areas.

*5 in.

Latin Sylvia undata | D. Provençaalse grasmus | F. Fauvette pitchou | G. Provencegrasmücke | S. Provencesångare

WILLOW-WARBLER

Small (11 cm*) slender greenish (above) and yellow (below) warbler
with lighter brownish legs than Chiffchaff, but otherwise very similar.
These birds can only be separated safely, by their quite different songs
Large trees are the usual song sites.

Small oven-like nest on the ground among grass; 6-7 eggs; May/June.
Incubation (13 d.) by female only; both parents feed young which fly
when about 2 w. old. Single- (double-) brooded.

Summer visitor (Apr./Sept.) breeding in fair numbers all over the
British Isles.

*4¼ in.

*Lat. Phylloscopus trochilus | D. Fitis | F. Pouillot fitis | G. Fitislaubvogel |
S. Lövsångare*

CHIFFCHAFF

Somewhat greyer above, and whiter below, than Willow-Warbler, always with blackish legs. Song of Chiffchaff (11 cm*), a monotonous chiff-chaff, repeated quite a few times, is characteristic.

Small oven-like nest near the ground in rank herbage or low bushes; 5-6 eggs; May/June. Only hen incubates (13 d.); both parents feed young that fly when about 2 w. old. Single- (double-) brooded.

Mainly summer visitor (Mch/Oct.) though few birds may winter in S. England, S. Wales and Ireland. Breeds in England (except Norfolk and NW. England) Wales and Ireland and locally, in S. Scotland.

*4¼ in.

Lat. Phylloscopus collybita | D. Tjiftjaf | F. Pouillot véloce | G. Weidenlaub-vogel | S. Gransångare

WOOD-WARBLER

Somewhat bigger (12½ cm*) than most other warblers, yellowish-green (above) and sulphur-yellow (throat and breast) and white (below) and bright-yellow stripe over the eye. Sexes alike.

Nest in hollow in the ground under undergrowth; 6-7 eggs; May/June. Incubation (12-13 d.) by hen only; both parents feed young which fly when 11-12 d. old. Single-brooded.

Summer visitor (Apr./Aug.) breeding in England and Wales, fairly common in S. Scotland but rare in Ireland. Has a distinct preference for beech woods, where its plaintive call gives away its presence.

*5 in.

Lat. Phylloscopus sibilatrix | D. Fluiter | F. Pouillot siffleur | G. Waldlaub-vogel | S. Grönsångare

GOLDCREST (left)

Tiniest (8½ cm*) of British birds with black-bordered yellow crest, orange in the centre in male and lemon-yellow in female (absent in juveniles). No black and white eye-stripes.

Nest is suspended from end of branch of conifer; 7-10 eggs; Apr./June. Only female incubates (14-16 d.), but both parents feed young which fly when about 3 w. old. Double-brooded.

Resident, though there is a southward movement in Autumn; breeding all over Britain (except Shetlands, Orkneys and O. Hebrides). British Goldcrests belong to the R.r. anglorum but the Continental race R.r. regulus passes along the E. coast.

*3½ in.

Lat. Regulus regulus | D. Goudhaantje | F. Roitelet huppé | G. Wintergold-hähnchen | S. Kungsfågel

FIRECREST (See ill. p. 252, right).

Same size (8½ cm*) and much like Goldcrest from which Firecrest can be surest told by black and white eye-stripes, though whole plumage is brighter and cleaner-looking. Orange-red in crown (brightest in male) is broader than in Goldcrest, with only small yellow seams. Young lack crest but have vague eye-stripes.

Winter visitor (Oct./Apr.) to English coast from Scilly Is. to Norfolk and less common to Kent, Sussex and Cornwall and to Wales.

Lat. Regulus ignicapillus | D. Vuurgoudhaantje | F. Roitelet à triple bandeau | G. Sommergoldhähnchen | S. Brandkronad kungsfågel

*3½ in.

PIED FLYCATCHER

Male black above with white under-parts and fore-head and broad white wing-bar (12½ cm*). Female and young very unobtrusive, but have typical flycatching-habit and white wing-bar (absent in Spotted Flycatcher.).

Nest in holes of trees, walls and in nest-boxes; 5-9 eggs; May/June. Incubation by hen only (12-13 d.); both parents feed young which fly when about 2 w. old. Single-brooded.

Summer-visitor and passage-migrant (Apr./Sept.) breeding in Wales, W. and N. England and S. Scotland and rare vagrant to Ireland.

*5 in.

L. Ficedula hypoleuca | D. Bonte vliegenvanger | F. Gobe-mouches noir | G. Trauerfliegenfänger | S. Svart och vit flugsnappare

SPOTTED FLYCATCHER

Unobtrusive bird (14 cm*) with habit of sitting upright on branch or fence-post making frequent sallies after insects and returning to the same perch. No wing-bars. Sexes alike.

Nest against walls or trees on some support; 4-5 eggs; May/June. Both sexes incubate (12-14 d.) and feed young which fly when about 2 w. old. Single- (double-) brooded.

Passage-migrant and summer visitor (Apr./Sept.) breeding all over Britain (though rarely in N. Scotland).

*5½ in.

Lat. Muscicapa striata | D. Grauwe vliegenvanger | F. Gobe-mouches gris | G. Grauer Fliegenfänger | S. Grå flugsnappare

HEDGE SPARROW

Sparrow-sized (14½ cm*) thin-billed with grey under-parts, streaked flanks and very vague wing-bar. Sexes alike.

Nest in hedges, evergreens or ivy; 4-5 eggs; Apr./June. Only hen incubates (12-13 d.); both parents feed young which fly when about 12 d. old. Two (three) broods.

Resident though birds from the N. move S. in autumn, breeding all over the British Isles (except Shetlands and scarce in the Orkneys). Hedge Sparrows in the Hebrides and W. Scotland have darker plumage (P.m. hebridium.)

*5¾ in.

Lat. Prunella modularis | Also: Dunnock | D. Heggemus | F. Accenteur mouchet | G. Heckenbraunelle | S. Järnsparv

MEADOW-PIPIT

Smaller (14½ cm*) but Sky-Lark-like bird, closely resembling Tree-Pipit, song being best field-mark.

Nest in depression in the ground between grasses; 3-5 eggs; Apr./June. Incubation (13-14 d.) chiefly by female; both parents feed young which fly when about 2 w. old. Double-brooded.

Partly resident though breeding birds leave N. in autumn and may even migrate to Ireland, France, Spain and Portugal. Many from the Continent pass through Britain or winter here.

*5¾ in.

Lat. Anthus pratensis | D. Graspieper | F. Pipit farlouse | G. Wiesenpieper | S. Ängpiplärka

Order *PASSERIFORMES*   Family *MOTACILLIDAE*

TREE-PIPIT

Slightly bigger (15 cm) than Meadow-Pipit. Likes perching in tops of trees from where it mounts steeply and parachutes down with wings and tail spread, singing all the time.

Nest in depression in the ground; 4-6 eggs; May/June. Incubation by hen only (13-14 d.); both parents feed young which fly when about 2 w. old. Single- (double-) brooded.

Summer visitor (Apr./Oct.) breeding in fair numbers in England (not W Cornwall), Wales and Scotland (not in the N.). Only vagrant in Ireland.
                                                                              *6 in.

Lat. Anthus trivialis | D. Boompieper | F. Pipit des arbres | G. Baumpieper | S. Trädpiplärka

ROCK-PIPIT

Still larger (15½ cm*) and darker pipit; outer tail-feathers are smoky-gray, not white.

Nest in hole of cliff; 4-5 eggs; Apr./June. Incubation (13-14 d.) by hen only; both parents feed young (fly when about 2 w. old). Double-brooded.

Rock-Pipit (A.s. petrosus) breeds along rocky shores of Britain, except O. Hebrides where slightly darker bird (A.s. meinertzhageni) breeds.

The WATER-PIPIT, winter visitor (Sept./Apr.) chiefly to SE. England, Wales and Ireland, has outer tail-feather pure white and whitish eye stripe.
                                                                              *6¼ in.

Lat. Anthus spinoletta | D. Rotspieper | F. Pipit maritime | G. Strandpieper | S. Skärpiplärka

PIED/WHITE WAGTAIL

Very slender (17½ cm* including tail) birds with black, grey and white plumage and black constantly wagging tails. Pied Wagtail has black back and rump, White Wagtail (illustrated) distinctly grey back and rump.

Nest in hole of wall, bank, shed, thatch or woodstack; 5-6 eggs; Apr./ July. Incubation (13-14 d.) chiefly by hen; both parents feed young which fly when about 2 w. old. Two (three) broods.

Pied Wagtail (M.a. yarrellii) is partly resident, breeding all over the British Isles. White Wagtail (M.a. alba) is chiefly coastal passage-migrant (occasional inland) from the Continent.

*7 in.

Lat. Motacilla alba | D. Rouwkwikstaart | Witte kwikstaart | F. Bergeronnette d' Yarrell | Bergeronnette grise | G. Trauerbachstelze | Bachstelze | S. Engelsk sädesärla | Sädesärla

Order PASSERIFORMES
Family MOTACILLIDAE

GREY WAGTAIL

Slightly bigger (17½ cm*) but otherwise much like Yellow Wagtail though longer tail, blue-grey upper-parts and greenish-yellow rump are distinctive. Male in spring has black throat.

Nest close to running water in hole or crevice; 4-6 eggs; Apr./June. Incubation (13-14 d.) chiefly by hen; both parents feed young which fly when about 2 w. old. Single-(double-) brooded.

Male (spring and summer)

Resident, breeding in England (scarce in E. and S.), Wales, Ireland and Scotland (scarce in N. and in the Orkneys and only visitor to the Shetlands and O. Hebrides) along swift running rocky streams.

Lat. Motacilla cinerea / D. Grote gele kwikstaart / F. Bergeronnette des ruisseaux / G. Bergbachstelze / S. Gråärla

*7 in.

YELLOW WAGTAIL

Male in spring has yellow head with crown and ear-coverts greenish (never bluish-grey) and yellow rump. Otherwise much like Blue-headed Wagtail (see picture on p. 260).

Nest in depression on the ground under cover; 5-6 eggs; May/June. Incubation (12-13 d.) and tending of young by both sexes. Young fly when about 2 w. old. Double- (single-) brooded.

Summer-visitor (Mch/Sept.) breeding in England and Wales (rarely in the W.) and Clyde-area of Scotland. Not in Ireland.

Lat. Motacilla flava flavissima / D. Engelse gele kwikstaart / F. Bergeronnette flavéole / G. Grünköpfige Schafstelze / S. Engelsk gulärla

BLUE-HEADED WAGTAIL

Only difference with Yellow Wagtail are bluish-grey crown and ear-coverts and white (not yellow) eye-stripe and chin. Females in autumn and immature birds are indistinguishable and intermediates occur.

The Blue-headed Wagtail breeds in small numbers in Sussex and Kent and has done so in several other counties, but is otherwise a passage-migrant through S. England. Inter-breeding accounts partly for intermediate plumages that can be very confusing.

Lat. Motacilla flava flava | D. Gele kwikstaart | F. Bergeronnette printanière | G. Schafstelze | S. Gulärla

RED-BACKED SHRIKE

Bigger than House-Sparrow (17½ cm*), male has blue-grey head, nape and rump and chestnut back with black stripe through eye. Female and young less distinctly coloured.

Nest in bushes and hedgerows, 5-6 eggs; May/June. Incubation (14-16 d.) by female only; both sexes feed young which fly when about 2 w. old. Single-brooded.

Passage-migrant and summer visitor (Apr./Oct.) breeding in fluctuating numbers in S. and central England and in Wales. Occasional visitor to Scotland and rare vagrant to Ireland.

*7 in.

Lat. Lanius collurio | D. Grauwe klauwier | F. Pie-grièche écorcheur | G. Rotrückenwürger | S. Vanlig törnskata

Order PASSERIFORMES 　　　　　　　　　　　　*Family STURNIDAE*

STARLING

Well-known and very common bird even in towns. Male plumage flecked in autumn, wearing off during winter and less prominent in females. Length about 21 cm*.

Tends to social nesting in holes of trees and buildings; 5-7 eggs; Apr./ June. Incubation (12-13 days) and tending of young which fly when about 3 w. old by both sexes. Single- (double-) brooded.

Resident breeding all over the British Isles though very local in W. Wales and W. Ireland. Many migrants from the Continent winter in Britain.

*8½ in.

Lat. Sturnus vulgaris / D. Spreeuw / F. Etourneau / G. Star / S. Stare

HAWFINCH

Rather big (16 cm*) heavy-billed stout finch with short white-tipped tail and obvious white patch on wings. Rather shy and very secretive bird. Sexes rather alike.

Nest usually on fruit-trees; 4-6 eggs; May/June. Only female incubates (9-10 d.); both parents feed young which fly when 10-12 d. old. One (two) broods.

Resident, breeding locally all over England, except in extreme west; rare in Wales and Scotland and only vagrant to Ireland.

*6½ in.

Lat. Coccothraustes coccothraustes | D. Appelvink | F. Gros-bec | G. Kirsch-kernbeisser | S. Stenknäck

263

GREENFINCH

Sparrow-sized (14½ cm*) olive-green finch with yellow patches on the wings and at sides of tail; yellow-green rump. Female somewhat duller, juveniles browner.

Nest in hedgerows or bushes; 4-6 eggs; Apr./ June. Only female incubates (13-14 d.); both parents feed young which fly when about 2 w. old. Two (three) broods.

Mainly resident, breeding commonly all over the British Isles, though only passage-migrant in Shetlands and O. Hebrides. Large numbers of passage-migrants and winter-visitors arrive on E. coast in autumn.

*5¾ in.

Lat. Chloris chloris | D. Groenling | F. Verdier | G. Grünling | S. Grönfink

GOLDFINCH

Small (12 cm*) finch with (adults) red face, conspicuous yellow bar on black wings and black white-tipped tail. Sexes alike. Juveniles lack red, white and black pattern of head but yellow wing-bar is distinctive.

Nests preferably on fruit-trees and chestnuts; 5-6 eggs; May/July. Incub. (12-13 d.) by hen only; both parents feed young which leave nest when about 2 w. old. Two (three) broods.

Rather common, though local resident, absent from most parts of Scottish Highlands.

*4¾ in.

Lat. Carduelis carduelis | D. Puttertje | F. Chardonneret | G. Stieglitz | S. Steglitsa

SISKIN

Smaller than House-Sparrow (12 cm*). Yellow-green, slender finch with black crown and chin and yellow rump. Female and juveniles duller and without black crown.

Nest in conifers; 3-5 eggs; Apr./June. Incubation (11-12 d.) by female only; both parents feed young which fly when about 2 w. old. Double-brooded.

Resident in Ireland and Scotland (though scarce in southern counties) and winter-visitor to England and Wales (Sept./Apr.).

*4¾ in.

Lat. Carduelis spinus | D. Sijsje | F. Tarin | G. Erlenzeisig | S. Grönsiska

LINNET

Slightly smaller than House-Sparrow ($13\frac{1}{2}$ cm*), male has chestnut mantle, grey head and (in summer only) red fore-head and breast. No black chin. Bill brown. Female and juveniles have no red and are duller coloured.

Nest in thorn-bushes or hedgerows; 4-6 eggs; Apr./June. Incubation chiefly by female (10-12 d.); both parents feed young which fly when 11-12 d. old. Two broods.

Mainly resident, breeding all over the British Isles. Winter visitors from the Continent.

*$5\frac{1}{4}$ in.

Lat. Carduelis cannabina | D. Kneu | F. Linotte mélodieuse | G. Bluthänfling | S. Hämpling

BULLFINCH

Fine male bird (14½ cm*) with black cap, red breast and under-parts, grey back and conspicuous white rump. Female has pinkish-grey under-parts. Juveniles are browner than female and lack black cap.

Nests preferably in thick hedges and evergreens; 4-5 eggs; May/June. Incubation chiefly by female (12-14 d.), but both parents feed young which fly when about 2 w. old. Two (three) broods.

Fairly common resident, though rather local in Scotland and Ireland, including the I. Hebrides. The race P.p. nesa is confined to the British Isles. The Northern bird P.p. pyrrhula, which is larger and more brightly coloured than our birds, is irregular autumn and winter visitor to E. coast (especially Scotland, the Shetlands and Fair Isle.)

*5¾ in.

*Latin. Pyrrhula pyrrhula /
D. Goudvink / F. Bouvreuil /
G. Gimpel / S. Domherre*

CHAFFINCH

Sparrow-sized (15 cm*). Male has blue crown and nape, chestnut mantle and pinkish-brown under-parts. Female and young far duller coloured. In flight both sexes have white shoulder-patch, white outer tail-feathers and green rump.

Nest in bushes or trees; 4-5 eggs; Apr./May. Incubation chiefly by hen (11-13 ins.); both parents feed young which fly when about 2 w. old. Single-brooded.

Resident, breeding in large numbers all over the British Isles (exceptionally Shetlands). Winter visitors F.c. coelebs (Scandinavia) and F.c. hortensis (Central Europe) are inseparable in the field.

*6 in.

Lat. Fringilla coelebs | D. (Boek)vink | F. Pinson des arbres | G. Buchfink | S. Bofink

Order PASSERIFORMES   *Family FRINGILLIDAE*

BRAMBLING

About same size (14½ cm*) as Chaffinch, with white rump and (in male) orange-buff shoulder-patch and breast; head brown or blackish. Female and juveniles are duller coloured. Often in flocks with other finches.

Winter-visitor in varying numbers (Sept./Apr.). Has bred exceptionally in Scotland.

*5¾ in.

Lat. Fringilla montifringilla | D. Keep | F. Pinson du Nord | G. Bergfink | S. Bergfink

CROSSBILL

This interesting finch (15 cm*) is distinctive on account of the tips of its beak crossing and which it uses to good effect in extracting seeds from fir cones. Male is red with brown wings and tail. Female olive-green and yellow, mottled with brown.

Nest in a fir tree; eggs 4-5; March/May. Incubation by female only (12-13 d.), young are fed by both parents. Single-(double-)brooded.

Resident in the north and irregularly in East Anglia and south-east England. Continental visitors may be seen on sporadic visits to any district where there are fir trees.

*6 in.

Latin. Loxia curvirostra | D. Kruisbek | F. Bec-croisé |
G. Fichtenkreuzschnabel | S. Mindre korsnäbb

YELLOW BUNTING

Front view

Order PASSERIFORMES
Family EMBERIZIDAE

YELLOW BUNTING

Buntings have longer tails than finches. Male Yellow-Hammer has yellow head and under-parts and chestnut mantle and rump. White outer tail-feathers. Female and juveniles duller coloured.

Nest on the ground at the foot of hedgerows and bushes; 3-4 eggs; Apr./June. Incubation chiefly by female (12-14 d.); both parents feed young which fly when about 12-13 d. old. Two broods.

Resident breeding all over the British Isles. Winter visitors from the Continent arrive at E. coast in Sept./Nov. and stay till Mch/Apr.

Lat. Emberiza citrinella | Also: Yellowhammer | D. Geelgors | F. Bruant jaune | G. Goldammer | S. Gulsparv

CORN-BUNTING

Large (17½ cm*) robust bunting with heavy head and bill. No white outer tail-feathers or wing-bar. Flies often with dangling legs. Song of male (from telegraph-poles or wires) characteristic. Sexes alike.

Nest on the ground or in low bushes; 3-5 eggs; May/June. Only hen incubates (12-13 d.) and male even seldom assists at feeding of young which fly already when 9-12 d. old. Single-(double-) brooded.

Partly resident, breeding (locally in fair numbers) in most parts of Britain. Part of our breeding birds emigrates in autumn and is replaced by winter-visitors from the Continent.

*7 in.

Lat. Emberiza calandra / D. Grauwe gors / F. Bruant proyer / G. Grauammer / S. Kornsparv

CIRL BUNTING

Smaller than Yellow Bunting (15 cm*) it has olive green tinge on breast and head. Cheeks are yellow with black band running through the eye. Throat black and underparts yellow and backbrown. White outer tail feathers seen in flight. Female lacks the black and yellow head.

Nest of grass, moss and hair low in bush; eggs 3-4; May/July; incubation by female only (12-14d.). Young (fed chiefly by female), fledge after 11-13 d. Two (three) broods.

Resident in the south only, where much rarer than Yellow Bunting.

*6 in.

Latin. Emberiza cirlus cirlus | D. Cirlgors | F. Bruant zizi | G. Zaunammer | S. Häcksparv

SNOW BUNTING

This is a white bird (15½ cm*) with black marking on tail and wings. Female has brown tinge. The note is a twitter and the birds may be seen in small flocks.

Nest among rocks made of grass, moss and feathers; eggs 4-6; May/July; incubation (12-14 d.) by female only (?), but both parents feed young which fledge after 10-12 d Single (double-) brooded.

Mainly winter visitor but breeds in small numbers in Scotland Mainly seen on high moorlands and the coast.

*6¼ in.

Latin. Plectrophenax nivalis / D. Sneeuwgors / F. Ortolan (or Bruant) de Neige / G. Schneeammer / S. Snösparv

REED-BUNTING

Sparrow-sized (15 cm*) bunting with characteristic black and white head-pattern (male) and white outer tail-feathers (both sexes).

Nest on or near the ground in marshy regions; 4-5 eggs; Apr./June. Incubation (13-14 d.) and feeding of young by both sexes. Two broods.

Present throughout the year though most birds move S. or even emigrate. Winter visitors from the Continent (Sept./Apr.). Breeds in most parts of of the British Isles.

*6 in.

Lat. Emberiza schoeniclus / D. Rietgors / F. Bruant de roseaux / G. Rohrammer / S. Sävsparv

Order PASSERIFORMES
Family PLOCEIDAE

HOUSE-SPARROW

Familiar bird (14½ cm*) to everyone, even townsmen. Male differs from Tree-Sparrow in having dark-grey crown and single white wing-bar. Female and juveniles have grey rump, no white shoulder-patch and no wing-bar.

Nest in all kinds of holes in or near houses; 3-4 eggs; May/Aug. (but may be found in any month). Incubation (12-14 d.) chiefly by hen; both parents feed young which fly when about 2 w. old. Two (three) broods.

Resident, breeding all over the British Isles though seldom far from human habitations. Local in many parts of Ireland.

*5¾ in.

Lat. Passer domesticus | D. Huismus | F. Moineau domestique | G. Haussperling | S. Gråsparv

TREE-SPARROW

Slightly smaller (14 cm*) than and somewhat resembling male House-Sparrow, but chocolate-brown crown, black patch on white cheeks and double white wing-bar are distinctive. Sexes alike.

Nest in holes of trees, buildings or cliffs; 4-6 eggs; Apr.-June. Incubation (12-14 d.) and tending of young (fly when 12-14 d. old) by both parents. Two (three) broods.

Resident, breeding locally in England and Scotland (rare in NW. and SW.) and Wales and even very local in some parts of Ireland.

*5½ in.

Lat. Passer montanus | D. Ringmus | F. Moineau friquet | G. Feldsperling | S. Pilfink

Above: Lesser Redpoll;
Below: Twite.

LESSER REDPOLL

Typical small finch (12½ cm*) of brownish colour with dark streaks, black chin and the distinct red forehead. It also has a pink breast and yellow bill. Juveniles lack red and pink colouring. Has the bounding flight of finches.

Breeds on heaths in spinneys and shrubberies and may be found in the outlying areas of towns. Eggs 4-6; May/June.

Resident over most of Britain. Gregarious, often joins with other finches in winter when visitors, including the larger Mealy Redpoll, arrive on the East Coast.

*5 in.

Lat. Carduelis flammea | D. KleineBarmsijs | F. Sizerin cabaret | G. Kleiner Birkenzeisig | S. Gråsiska

TWITE

Also known as Mountain Linnet. A small member of finch family (13 cm*). Brown with dark streaks and pink rump. Bill grey in summer and yellow in winter. Buff-coloured under chin. Closely resembles juvenile linnet. Has bounding flight of the finches and shows white on wing. Gregarious and often flocks with other finches.

Eggs 4-6: May/June.

Resident mostly in north part of Britain and breeds on heather and open ground. Winter visitors arrive S. and E. England.

*5¼ in.

Latin. Carduelis flavirostris | D. Fratertje | F. Linotte à bec jaune | G. Berghänfling | S. Gulnäbbad hämpling

281

HAWFINCH

NOTES

The two birds on pages 249 and 250 present one of the outstanding puzzles of bird watching for the Willow-Warbler and the Chiff-chaff are so similar that it is only an experienced eye which can separate them. The one sure method of identification is their song. The Willow Warbler has a more gently fluent series of descending notes whilst the other bird calls a continuous "chiff-chaff" which can never be mistaken. Both sing from a large tall tree.

The Goldcrest is a delight, it being the tiniest of the British birds; its nest is suspended from a connifer branch and is one of those features of bird life which never fails to charm. The Pipits are also birds which can be distinguished by their song; it is uttered as they leave and return to the ground. They also have the Wagtails' nimble run.

The Wagtails are to be seen everywhere and their striking plumage makes them unmistakable. The habits of the Starling are full of interest, it is indeed a fascinating bird to watch. It has been called the "English Mocking Bird" for it can mimic other birds and can command an extraordinary repertoire.

Finally, there are the Finches which are the most numerous birds, the Chaffinch is believed to have the greatest population, whilst the Sparrow is every where in town and country. The Hawfinch, Goldfinch, Bullfinch and Crossbill are among the most handsome of the small birds and being resident they are some of our closest friends.

CLASSIFICATION

Present-day systems of classification aim at showing how, in the course of evolution, one form has developed from another. However, the tree of life is three-dimensional and it is not possible to put it in two-dimensional print. Also, taxonomists, who are the scientists that work in this special branch of ornithology, do not always agree on details. The Species is the only biological reality with which they work; all other categories being man-made are, therefore, subjective groupings. Even modern books on birds do not always agree upon details.

R. E. Moreau, President of the British Ornithologists' Union, has suggested that it might be better 'to drop pretences' and arrange the Species alphabetically within the Genus, the Genera within the Family or Sub-family, the Families within the Sub-orders and the Sub-orders within the Orders. For practical reasons only he would maintain the present arrangement of the Orders, on which there is general agreement. Rightly Moreau points out that other branches of zoology are using the alphabetical arrangement to an increasing extent, but so far this suggestion seems to be too revolutionary. The *New Dictionary of Birds*, published in 1964 by the B.O.U. still follows the system of the late J. L. Peters' 'Check-list of the Birds of the World', based on Wetmore.

As it is desirable to standardise one particular system, I should have liked to follow the arrangement of the *New Dictionary* but for technical reasons of printing this has not been possible. However, for those who take an interest in this subject, the following is the arrangement as presented in the *New Dictionary*, restricting it to the birds that are dealt with in BIRD SPOTTING.

	Family
Order GAVIIFORMES	Gaviidae
Order PODICIPEDIFORMES	Podicipitidae
Order PROCELLARIIFORMES	Procellariidae
	Hydrobatidae
Order PELECANIFORMES	
Suborder Pelecani	
Superfamily Suloidea	Sulidae
	Phalacrocoracidae
Order CICONIIFORMES	
Suborder Ardeae	Ardeidae
Suborder Ciconiae	
Superfamily Ciconicidea	Ciconiidae
Superfamily	
Threskiornithoidea	Threskiornithidae
Order ANSERIFORMES	
Suborder Anseres	Anatidae
Order FALCONIFORMES	
Suborder Falcones	Accipitridae
	Falconidae
Order GALLIFORMES	
Suborder Galli	
Superfamily Phasianoidea	Tetraonidae
	Phasianidae
Order GRUIFORMES	
Suborder Grues	
Superfamily Ralloidea	Rallidae
Order CHARADRIIFORMES	
Suborder Charadrii	Haematopodidae
	Charadriidae
	Scolopacidae
	Recurvirostridae
	Phalaropodidae
Suborder Lari	Stercorariidae
	Laridae

	Family
Suborder Alcae	Alcidae
Order COLUMBIFORMES	
Suborder Columbae	Columbidae
Order CUCULIFORMES	
Suborder Cuculi	Cuculidae
Order STRIGIFORMES	Tytonidae
	Strigidae
Order CAPRIMULGIFORMES	
Suborder Caprimulgi	Caprimulgidae
Order APODIFORMES	
Suborder Apodi	Apodidae
Order CORACIIFORMES	
Suborder Alcedines	
Superfamily Alcedinoidea	Alcedinidae
Suborder Coracii	Upupidae
Order PICIFORMES	
Suborder Pici	Picidae
Order PASSERIFORMES	
Suborder Oscines	Alaudidae
	Hirundinidae
	Motacillidae
	Laniidae
	Bombycillidae
	Cinclidae
	Troglodytidae
	Prunellidae
	Muscicapidae
	Subfamily Turdinae
	Subfamily Sylviinae
	Subfamily Muscicapinae
	Paridae
	Sittidae
	Certhiidae
	Emberizidae
	Fringillidae
	Ploceidae
	Sturnidae
	Oriolidae
	Corvidae

INDEX (ENGLISH NAMES)

INDEX (LATIN NAMES)

RECORDED BIRD SONGS

The Royal Society for the Protection of Birds, The Lodge, Sandy, Beds., issues a series of bird song records entitled "Listen—the Birds". They are as follows:-

1 Blackbird; Song Trush; Mistle Thrush; Golden Oriole; Robin; Cuckoo; Nuthatch; Wood Pigeon; Jay.

2 Garden Warbler; Blackcap; Wren; Wood Warbler; Chiffchaff; Firecrest; Goldcrest; Coal Tit; Marsh Tit; Great Tit.

3 Nightingale; Willow Warbler; Whitethroat; Icterine Warbler; Great Reed Warbler; Reed Warbler; Marsh Warbler; Grasshopper Warbler.

4 Tawny Owl; Little Owl; Scops Owl; Long-eared Owl; Barn Owl; Wryneck; Green Woodpecker; Grey-headed Woodpecker; Great Spotted Woodpecker; Black Woodpecker.

5 Skylark; Woodlark; Tree Pipit; Hoopoe; Redstart; Black Redstart; Swallow; Sand Martin.

6 Starling; Pied Flycatcher; Serin; Redbacked Shrike; Whinchat; Reed Bunting; Nightjar; Turtle Dove.

7 Dunnock; House Sparrow; Tree Sparrow; Greenfinch; Goldfinch; Chaffinch; Lesser Redpoll; Linnet; Twite; Corn Bunting; Yellowhammer.

8 Common Sandpiper; Snipe; Woodcock; Golden Plover; Curlew; Lapwing; Oystercatcher; Redshank; Wader Chorus.

9 Seabird Colony; Herring Gull; Lesser Black-backed Gull; Great Black-backed Gull; Common Gull; Black-headed Gull; Common Tern; Rock Pipit; Meadow Pipit; Chorus of Gulls.

10 Mallard; Gadwall; Shoveler; Teal; Wigeon; Pochard; Shelduck; Canada Goose; Mute Swan; Whooper Swan; Little Grebe; Red-throated Diver.

11 Red Grouse; Blackcock; Dunlin; Wheatear; Stonechat; Ring Ouzel; Spotted Flycatcher; Pied Wagtail; Yellow Wagtail; Grey Wagtail; Corncrake.

12 Swift; House Martin; Blue Tit; Tree Creeper; Carrion Crow; Rook; Jackdaw; Magpie; Kittiwake; Sandwich Tern.

Printed in The Netherlands by 'The Ysel Press' Deventer